TRUE COLORS

An EFL Course for Real Communication

1

Jay Maurer
Irene E. Schoenberg

Joan Saslow
Series Director

Longman

**True Colors: An EFL Course for Real
Communication 1**

Pearson Education, 10 Bank Street, White Plains, NY 10606

Senior acquisitions editor: Allen Ascher
Director of design and production: Rhea Banker
Senior production editor: Linda Moser
Cover design: Rhea Banker
Text design: Word & Image Design
Text composition: Word & Image Design
Illustrations: Pierre Berthiaume, Jocelyn Bouchard, Eric Colquhoun,
    Brian Hughes, Don Kilby, Paul McCusker, Dusan Petricic,
    Quack Communications, Stephen Quinlan, Richard Row,
    Steve Shulman, Teco, Margot Thompson, Angela Vaculik
Photography: Gilbert Duclos

Library of Congress Cataloging-in-Publication Data

Maurer, Jay.
    True colors: an EFL course for real communication/Jay Maurer; Irene E.
    Schoenberg; Joan Saslow, series director
        p. cm.
    ISBN 0-201-87808-9
    1. English language—Textbooks for foreign speakers.
2. Communication.   I. Schoenberg, Irene.   II. Saslow, Joan M.   III. Title.

PE1128.M3548   1998

428.2′4–dc21   97-12071
                                                      CIP

12 13 14 —CRK—07 06 05 04 03

Contents

●●

Scope and Sequence   iv

Acknowledgments   vi

Preface   vii

Unit 1 • Are you in this class?   2

Unit 2 • There's a noise downstairs!   14

Unit 3 • For computer questions, press one now.   26

Unit 4 • What's Bob doing?   38

Unit 5 • You lose it. We find it.   50

Units 1–5 • Review, SelfTest, and Extra Practice   62

Unit 6 • We're going to win.   72

Unit 7 • Can you dance?   84

Unit 8 • Do you want some pizza, Lulu?   96

Unit 9 • Weren't you at Alice's?   108

Unit 10 • My plane just landed.   120

Units 6–10 • Review, SelfTest, and Extra Practice   132

Activity Links   144

Appendices   146

   Key Vocabulary   146

   Simple Past Tense of Irregular Verbs   150

   Irregular Noun Plurals   150

   Spelling Rules for the Present Participle   150

Scope and Sequence of Specific Content and Skills

UNIT	Social Language	Vocabulary	Grammar	Listening
1 Are you in this class? page 2	How to: • make informal introductions • talk about occupations • ask questions / make negative statements • describe people	• nouns for talking about people • occupations • nouns and adjectives that describe people	• verb *be*--use and form • subject pronouns • contractions • indefinite and definite articles	Type: • a TV quiz program Comprehension Skill: • focus attention
2 There's a noise downstairs! page 14	How to: • say the time • identify yourself on the phone / ask how someone is • make plans to meet • describe things and places	• telling time • prepositions for times of the day and dates	• count and non-count nouns: *there is/there are*	Types: • a recorded announcement • a phone conversation Comprehension Skills: • focus attention • determine context
3 For computer questions, press one now. page 26	How to: • suggest an activity/an alternative • state address / phone number • describe family relationships	• social activities • machines and appliances • family relationships • classroom commands	• commands • suggestions with *let's* • possessive adjectives • possessive nouns	Type: • a voice mail message Comprehension Skill: • focus attention
4 What's Bob doing? page 38	How to: • talk about actions in progress • apologize • offer to call back later • give directions to a place • talk about order	• everyday activities • ordinal numbers • locations and directions	• the present continuous • object pronouns	Type: • a phone conversation Comprehension Skill: • determine context
5 You lose it. We find it. page 50	How to: • talk about work • ask about and express likes • talk about studies • express dislikes • talk about habitual activities	• places to work • fields of study • adjectives to describe studies	• the simple present tense	Types: • a photo story • a story about detectives • a conversation in an office Comprehension Skills: • confirming content • determine context • focus attention
Review of Units 1–5 page 62				
6 We're going to win. page 72	How to: • make an appointment • talk about pains / illnesses • describe plans • talk about frequency • describe feelings	• parts of the body • general locations • aches, pains, and illnesses • frequency adverbs	• the future with *be going to* • placement of frequency adverbs	Types: • interviews Comprehension Skills: • determine context • focus attention
7 Can you dance? page 84	How to: • express obligations / regrets • make invitations with *let's* • ask for help • express gratitude • talk about ability	• leisure activities • academic subjects	• *have to / has to* • *can*	Types: • conversations Comprehension Skills: • determine context • focus attention
8 Do you want some pizza, Lulu? page 96	How to: • get someone's attention • ask about price • agree to buy • state a need • express disbelief	• clothing • colors	• *some* and *any* • *one* and *ones* • *this, that, these,* and *those*	Types: • a photo story • a conversation Comprehension Skills: • factual recall • focus attention
9 Weren't you at Alice's? page 108	How to: • talk about the past • give and accept an apology • confirm identity • talk about ownership and possession	• past time expressions • social and business relationships	• the past tense of *be* • possessive pronouns	Type: • a telephone conversation Comprehension Skills: • focus attention
10 My plane just landed. page 120	How to: • talk about past actions and facts • talk about recent activities • empathize	• more past time expressions	• the simple past tense of regular and irregular verbs	Type • an extended dialogue Comprehension Skill: • determine context
Review of Units 6–10 page 132				

Reading	Writing	Pronunciation	Expression of Opinions
Types: • a photo story • a newspaper article Comprehension Skills: • confirming content • factual recall	Task: • addressing an envelope Skill: • capitalization of names of people and places	• the alphabet	• opinions of occupations and studies
Types: • a photo story • short paragraphs Comprehension Skills: • factual recall • identifying the main idea	Task: • a short note to a classmate Skill • period and question mark	• /s/, /z/, and /iz/	• favorite places
Types: • a photo story • advertisements Comprehension Skills: • confirming content • factual recall	Type: • phone messages Skill: • writing names, times, and phone numbers	• stress and meaning	• value of certain machines and appliances
Types: • a photo story • an extended dialogue Comprehension Skills: • confirming content • drawing conclusions	Type: • a letter Skill: • spelling present participles	• /iʸ/ and /i/	• opinions about lateness
Type: • an extended dialogue Comprehension Skills: • identifying the main idea	Type: • note taking Skill: • writing the simple present tense	• /s/, /z/, and /iz/	• tastes in foods, people, music, etc.
Types: • a photo story • an extended dialogue Comprehension Skills: • drawing conclusions • interpretation and analysis	Type: • a business letter Skill: • a formal letter style	• intonation of questions	• good and bad ways to meet people • opinions about meeting and dating
Types: • a photo story • an essay Comprehension Skills: • confirming content • factual recall	Type: • a student newspaper article Skill: • developing paragraphs	• *can* and *can't* in sentences (stressed and unstressed)	• reasons why people like or dislike dancing
Type: • an extended dialogue Comprehension Skill: • interpretation and analysis	Type: • an extended dialogue Skills: • use of colon in dialogue style • writing questions in the simple present tense and the present continuous	• /ɑ/ and /ʌ/	• problems between parents and children • how can families communicate better?
Types: • a photo story • an extended dialogue Comprehension Skills: • confirming content • understanding meaning from context	Type: • a paragraph about dating Skill: • development of a topic sentence	• the /r/ and /h/ sounds • the /r/ and /l/ sounds • the /r/, /d/ , and /t/ sounds	• who pays on a date?
Types: • a photo story • a magazine article Comprehension Skills: • factual recall • understanding meaning from context	Type: • a description of a person Skill: • writing facts about the past	• past tense endings: *worked / played / repeated*	• environment vs. heredity

Acknowledgments

●●●●●●●●●●●●●●●●●●●●●●●●●●●●●

The authors and series director wish to acknowledge with gratitude the following consultants, reviewers, and piloters—our partners in the development of *True Colors*.

Consultants

Berta de Llano, Puebla, Mexico • **Luis Fernando Gómez J.**, School of Education, University of Antioquia, Colombia • **Irma K. Ghosn**, Lebanese American University, Byblos, Lebanon • **Annie Hu**, Fu-Jen Catholic University, Taipei, Taiwan • **Nancy Lake**, CEL-LEP, São Paulo, Brazil • **Frank Lambert**, Pagoda Foreign Language Institute, Seoul, Korea • **Kazuhiko Yoshida**, Kobe University, Kobe City, Japan.

Reviewers and Piloters

• **Lucia Adrian**, EF Language Schools, Miami, Florida, USA • **Ronald Aviles**, Instituto Chileno Norteamericano, Chuquicamata, Chile • **Liliana Baltra**, Instituto Chileno Norteamericano, Santiago, Chile • **Paulo Roberto Berkelmans**, CEL-LEP, São Paulo, Brazil • **Luis Beze**, Casa Thomas Jefferson, Brasília, Brazil • **Martin T. Bickerstaff**, ELS Language Centers, Oakland, California, USA • **Mary C. Black**, Institute of North American Studies, Barcelona, Spain • **James Boyd**, ECC Foreign Language Institute, Osaka, Japan • **Susan Bryan de Martínez**, Instituto Mexicano Norteamericano, Monterrey, Mexico • **Hugo A. Buitano**, Instituto Chileno Norteamericano, Arica, Chile • **Gary Butzbach**, American Language Center, Rabat, Morocco • **Herlinda Canto**, Universidad Popular Autónoma del Estado de Puebla, Mexico • **Rigoberto Castillo**, Colegio de CAFAM, Santafé de Bogotá, Colombia • **Tina M. Castillo**, Santafé de Bogotá, Colombia • **Amparo Clavijo Olarte**, Universidad Distrital, Santafé de Bogotá, Colombia • **Graciela Conocente**, Asociación Mendocina de Intercambio Cultural Argentino Norteamerica, Argentina • **Greg Conquest**, Yokohama Gaigo Business College, Japan • **Eduardo Corbo**, IETI, Salto, Uruguay • **Marilia Costa**, Instituto Brasil-Estados Unidos, Rio de Janeiro, Brazil • **Miles Craven**, Nihon University, Shizuoka, Japan • **Michael Davidson**, EF Language Schools, Miami, Florida, USA • **Celia de Juan**, UNICO, UAG, Guadalajara, Mexico • **Laura de Marín**, Centro Colombo Americano, Medellín, Colombia • **Montserrat Muntaner Djmal**, Instituto Brasil-Estados Unidos, Rio de Janeiro, Brazil • **Deborah Donnelley de García**, ITESM-Campus Querétaro, Mexico • **Rosa Erlichman**, União Cultural, São Paulo, Brazil • **Patricia Escalante Arauz**, Universidad de Costa Rica, San Pedro de Montes de Oca, Costa Rica • **Guadalupe Espinoza**, ITESM-Campus Querétaro, Mexico • **Suad Farkouh**, ESL Consultant to Philadelphia National Schools, Amman, Jordan • **Niura R.H. Ferreria**, Centro Cultural Brasil Estados Unidos, Guarapuava, Brazil • **Fernando Fleurquin**, Alianza Cultural Uruguay-EEUU, Montevideo, Uruguay • **Patricia Fleury**, Casa Thomas Jefferson, Brasília, Brazil • **Patricia Foncea**, Colegio Jesualdo, Santiago, Chile • **Areta Ulhana Galat**, Centro Cultural Brasil Estados Unidos, Curitiba, Brazil• **Christina Gitsaki**, Nagoya University of Commerce and Business Administration, Japan • **Julie Harris de Peyré**, Universidad del Valle, Guatemala • **Ruth Hassell de Hernández**, UANL, Mexico • **Mia Kim**, Kyung Hee University, Seoul, Korea • **John Hawkes**, EF International School, Santa Barbara, California, USA •

Rose M. Hernández, University of Puerto Rico-Bayamón, Puerto Rico • **Susan Hills**, EF International School of English, San Diego, California, USA • **Jan Kelley**, EF International School, Santa Barbara, California, USA • **Junko Kobayashi**, Sankei International College, Tokyo, Japan • **Gil Lancaster**, Academy Istanbul, Istanbul, Turkey • **Mónica Lobo**, Santiago, Chile • **Luz Adriana Lopera**, Centro Colombo Americano, Medellín, Colombia • **Eva Irene Loya**, ITESM-Campus Querétaro, Mexico • **Mary Maloy Lara**, Instituto John F. Kennedy, Tehuacán, Mexico • **Meire de Jesus Marion**, Associação Alumni, São Paulo, Brazil • **Juliet Marlier**, Universidad de las Américas, Puebla, Mexico • **Yolanda Martínez**, Instituto D'Amicis, Puebla, Mexico • **Neil McClelland**, Shimonoseki City University, Japan • **Regina Celia Pereira Mendes**, Instituto Brasil-Estados Unidos, Rio de Janeiro, Brazil • **Jim Miller**, Yokohama Gaigo Business College, Japan • **Fiona Montarry**, The American Language Center, Casablanca, Morocco • **Luiz Claudio Monteiro**, Casa Thomas Jefferson, Brasília, Brazil • **Angelita Oliveira Moreno**, ICBEU, Belo Horizonte, Brazil • **Ahmed Mohammad Motala**, King Fahd University of Petroleum & Minerals, Dhahran, Saudi Arabia • **William Richard Munzer**, Universidad IDEAS de Bogotá, Colombia • **Akiko Nakazawa**, Yokohama Gaigo Business College, Japan • **Adrian Nunn**, EF International School of English, Los Angeles, California, USA • **Margarita Ordaz Mejía**, Universidad Americana de Acapulco, Mexico • **Sherry Ou**, Fu-Jen Catholic University, Taipei, Taiwan • **Thelma Jonas Péres**, Casa Thomas Jefferson, Brasília, Brazil • **Renata Philippov**, Associação Alumni, São Paulo, Brazil • **Ciaran Quinn**, Otemae College, Osaka, Japan • **Ron Ragsdale**, Bilgi University, Istanbul, Turkey • **Luis Ramírez F.**, Instituto Norteamericano de Cultura, Concepción, Chile • **Martha Restrepo Rodríguez**, Politécnico Grancolombiano, Santafé de Bogotá, Colombia • **Irene Reyes Giordanelli**, Centro Cultural Colombo Americano, Santiago de Cali, Colombia • **Dolores Rodríguez**, CELE (Centro de Lenguas), Universidad Autónoma de Puebla, Mexico • **Idia Rodríguez**, University of Puerto Rico-Arecibo, Puerto Rico • **Eddy Rojas & teachers**, Centro de Idiomas de la P. Universidad Católica, Peru • **Ricardo Romero**, Centro Cultural Colombo Americano, Santafé de Bogotá, Colombia • **Blanca Lilia Rosales Bremont**, Universidad Americana de Acapulco, Mexico • **Marie Adele Ryan**, Associação Alumni, São Paulo, Brazil • **Nadia Sarkis**, União Cultural, São Paulo, Brazil • **Andrea Seidel**, Universidad Americana de Acapulco, Mexico • **Hada Shammar**, American Language Center, Amman, Jordan • **Lai Yin Shem**, Centro Colombo Americano, Medellín, Colombia • **Maria Cristina Siqueira**, CEL-LEP, São Paulo, Brazil • **María Inés Sandoval Astudillo**, Instituto Chileno Norteamericano, Chillán, Chile • **Lilian Munhoz Soares**, Centro Cultural Brasil Estados Unidos, Santos, Brazil • **Mário César de Sousa**, Instituto Brasil-Estados Unidos, Fortaleza, Brazil • **Tatiana Suárez**, Politécnico Grancolombiano, Santafé de Bogotá, Colombia • **Richard Paul Taylor**, Nagoya University of Commerce and Business Administration, Japan • **David Thompson**, Instituto Mexicano Norteamericano de Relaciones Culturales, Guadalajara, Mexico • **Yoshihiro Uzawa**, Sankei International College, Tokyo, Japan • **Nilda Valdez**, Centro Cultural Salvadoreño, El Salvador • **Euclides Valencia Cepeda**, Universidad Distrital, Santafé de Bogotá, Colombia • **Ana Verde**, American Language Institute, Montevideo, Uruguay • **Andrea Zaidenberg**, Step English Language Center, Argentina

Preface

True Colors is a complete and articulated five-level adult or young adult course in English as a foreign language. Each book is intended to be completed in a period of 60 to 90 class hours. There are two possible beginning-level entry points: Basic level or Book 1.

There are two reasons why this course is entitled *True Colors*. It presents the true voice of the native speaker of American English, and it systematically teaches students to communicate *in their own words*—to **let their true colors shine through.**

Focus and Approach

True Colors is a highly communicative international course enhanced by strong four-skills support, including a two-step listening strand and an abundance of games, info-gaps, and other interactive activities. Within each unit short, integrated social language and grammar lessons ensure concentrated oral practice and production. *True Colors* takes into account different learning and teaching styles. It is centered on task-based strategies and the well-known fact that practice in each skill area enhances mastery of the others.

A major innovation of the *True Colors* series is to systematically build students' ability to present their own ideas, opinions, and feelings—both accurately and confidently. For this reason, every activity leads students to gain ownership of the language, progressively moving them *away* from models

to express thoughts in their own words and to improvise based on what they know.

True Colors carefully distinguishes between receptive and productive language. It consistently presents language in the receptive mode before—and at a slightly higher difficulty level than—the productive mode. Research has shown that students are more successful when they become familiar with new language before having to produce it. For this reason, *True Colors* presents EFL students with a wealth of both receptive and productive models, combining exposure and practice for increased understanding and attainable mastery.

True Colors is specifically designed for use by students who rarely encounter English outside of class. The course is built around a wealth of speaking and reading models of the true voice of the American speaker. This refreshing change from "textbook English" is essential for students who have limited access to real native speech and writing.

Because international students do not have the opportunity to speak to native speakers on a regular basis, *True Colors* does not present activities such as interviewing native speakers or watching TV in English. Instead, the course serves as a replacement for immersion in an English-speaking environment, making the classroom itself a microcosm of the English-speaking world. The goal and promise of *True Colors* is to prepare students to move out of this textbook and to understand, speak, read, and write in the real world.

Student Population

Book 1 of *True Colors* is written for adult and young adult false beginners. It has been pilot-tested in classrooms throughout the world and with students of numerous language groups.

Book 4 concludes at a high-intermediate level. The Basic level text is an alternative entry point for very weak false beginners or true beginners.

Course Length

The *True Colors* Student's Books are designed to cover from 60 to 90 class hours of instruction. Although each Student's Book is a complete course in itself, giving presentation, practice, and production of all four skills, a full complement of supplementary materials is available to further expand the material.

Components of the Course

Student's Book   The student's book is made up of ten units and two review units, one coming after unit five and another coming after unit ten.

Teacher's Edition   The teacher's edition is interleaved with full-color student's book pages and contains an introduction to the format and approach of *True Colors;* page-by-page teaching suggestions especially written for the teacher who teaches outside an English-speaking country; tapescripts for the audiocassettes; a complete answer key to the exercises in the student's book, workbook, and achievement tests.

Teacher's Bonus Pack   The Teacher's Bonus Pack is a unique set of reproducible

hands-on learning-support activities that includes flash cards for large- or small-group vocabulary presentations, pronunciation game cards, duplicating masters that contain photo stories with empty speech balloons for student oral and written improvisation, learner-created grammar notes, and interactive conversation cards for social language reinforcement. The Teacher's Bonus Pack provides suggestions for tailoring *True Colors* to the needs of a variety of settings.

Workbook   The workbook contains numerous additional opportunities for written reinforcement of the language taught in the student's book. The exercises in the workbook are suitable for homework or for classwork.

Audiocassettes   The audiocassettes contain all the receptive models for listening and reading, the conversations, the vocabulary presentations, the Listening with a Purpose texts, the reading texts, and the pronunciation presentations and practices from the student's book. The audiocassettes provide space for student practice and self-correction.

Videocassette   The videocassette, *True Voices,* contains a unique combination of controlled and improvised dramatic episodes that support the social language and grammar in the *True Colors* student's book. In addition, students see a video magazine of scenes depicting the themes touched on throughout the student's book (shopping, working, etc.) and on-the-street interviews about the same topics and themes.

Video Workbook   A video workbook provides active language practice and reinforcement of all social language and grammar from the video.

Achievement Tests   Achievement tests offer opportunities for evaluation of student progress on a unit-by-unit basis. In addition, a placement test is available to aid in placing groups in one of the five levels of *True Colors:* Basic, Book 1, Book 2, Book 3, or Book 4.

Student's Book Unit Contents

Photo Story   An illustrated conversation or story provokes interest, provides enjoyment, and demonstrates the use of target language in authentic, natural speech. This rich model of real speech can be presented as a reading or a listening. It is purposely designed to be a slight step ahead of students' productive ability because students can understand more than they can produce, and the EFL student needs abundant authentic models of native speech.

Comprehension   Questions about the conversation focus on the key comprehension skills of factual recall, confirmation of content, identifying main ideas, drawing conclusions, and understanding meaning from context. These can serve as listening comprehension or reading comprehension exercises.

Social Language and Grammar Lessons Short, numbered lessons form the instructional core of each unit of *True Colors.* Social language and grammar are tightly linked in each of these mini-lessons, through the following combination of presentations and opportunities for practice:

Conversation   A short dialogue at the students' productive level presents and models important social language.

Pair Practice   The same dialogue is presented for student practice with opportunities for personalization of the social language. This limited opportunity for manipulation is the first step toward ownership of the language that is the goal and promise of *True Colors* .

Vocabulary   Illustrated and captioned vocabulary presentations within each unit provide students with important words to make their own. Students are not asked to guess the meaning of the unit's active vocabulary; instead, *True Colors* presents a clear illustration to convey meaning and follows it with opportunities for practice and free production.

Grammar   Clear, well-explained grammar presentations are integrated with the social language and support comprehension and production of it. These grammar presentations never occur in isolation but rather form a support for the social language of the lesson, giving the grammar both meaning and purpose. To this end, grammar exercises are set in a context that supports the communicative focus of the lesson.

A major goal of *True Colors* is to teach students to improvise based on the language they already know. Improvisation is the "fifth skill"—the one students need to master in order to move out of the pages of a textbook and into the real world. Through a continuum of freer and freer opportunities for language ownership, *True Colors* students put the course into their own words, **letting their own true colors shine through.**

Pronunciation   Each unit isolates a basic and important feature of the pronunciation or intonation of spoken American English. Practice is structured into games and into listening, speaking, and dictation activities.

Game or Info-Gap   Each unit contains at least one interactive language activity that activates grammar, social language, vocabulary, or pronunciation.

Listening with a Purpose   In addition to the recorded texts in the unit, one or two additional listening texts provide another receptive model a step above students' productive ability. A two-step comprehension syllabus centers on two essential listening skills—determining context and focusing attention. Through a unique and rigorous approach to listening comprehension similar to the reading comprehension skills of skimming and scanning, students build their ability to understand at a level above what is normally expected of false beginners.

Reading   Each unit provides practice in the reading skill with texts slightly above students' productive ability. Topics are especially devised to create motivated readers, and each reading is followed by further comprehension practice in all the comprehension sub skills.

   This unique and exciting culminating activity systematically builds students' ability to express their own opinions, ideas, and feelings on a variety of topics. Carefully designed questions provoke interest without soliciting production above students' level. Each Heart to Heart activity comes near the end of the unit, ensuring adequate preparation for success.

Writing   Writing activities in each unit provide real and realistic writing tasks that reinforce the target language in the writing skill while providing additional opportunities for personal expression.

   This full-page illustration ends each unit and has been especially drawn to elicit from students all the language they have learned within the unit—the vocabulary, the social language, the grammar, and the thematic contexts. Students begin talking about the contents of this picture early in the unit and continue throughout the unit. At the end of the unit, they ask each other questions about the actions depicted, they make true and false statements about what they see, they create conversations for the characters, they tell stories about what is happening—all IN THEIR OWN WORDS. All students, regardless of ability, will succeed at their own levels because what the students know how to say has been drawn into the illustration and what they don't know how to say has been purposely left out.

Review units   These units are provided after unit five (mid-book) and at the end. They provide review, self-tests, extra classroom practice, and a social language self-test.

Appendices   The key vocabulary, spelling rules, and noun and verb charts are organized and presented at the end of the book for easy reference and test preparation.

About the Authors and Series Director

Authors

Jay Maurer

Jay Maurer has taught English in Binational Centers, colleges, and universities in Portugal, Spain, Mexico, the Somali Republic, and the United States. In addition, he taught intensive English at Columbia University's American Language Program.

Dr. Maurer has an M.A. and an M. Ed. in Applied Linguistics as well as a Ph. D. in The Teaching of English, all from Columbia University. In addition to this new adult and young adult English course, he is the author of the Advanced Level of Longman's widely acclaimed *Focus on Grammar* series and co-author of the three-level *Structure Practice in Context* series. Dr. Maurer teaches and writes in the Seattle, Washington, area and recently conducted a series of teaching workshops in Brazil and Japan.

Irene E. Schoenberg

Irene E. Schoenberg has taught English to international students for over twenty years at Hunter College's International Language Institute and at Columbia University's American Language Program. Additionally, she trains English instructors in EFL/ESL teaching methods at The New School for Social Research. Her M.A. is in TESOL from Columbia University. She is a popular speaker to national and international TESOL groups.

Professor Schoenberg is the author of the Basic Level of the *Focus on Grammar* series as well as the author of the two engaging, unique, and widely-used conversation texts, *Talk About Trivia* and *Talk About Values.* In addition to *True Colors,* Professor Schoenberg is developing a new visual dictionary for learners of English.

Series Director

Joan Saslow

Joan Saslow has taught English and foreign languages to adults and young adults in both South America and the United States. She taught English at the Binational Centers of Valparaíso and Viña del Mar, Chile, and English and French at the Catholic University of Valparaíso. She taught English as a Foreign Language to Japanese university students at Marymount College and to international students in Westchester Community College's intensive program.

Ms. Saslow is the author of *English in Context: Reading Comprehension for Science and Technology,* a three-level text series. In addition, Ms. Saslow has been an editor of language teaching materials, a teacher trainer, and a frequent speaker at gatherings of English teachers outside the United States for twenty-five years.

Are you in this class?

Warm up: *Look at the pictures. Where are these people—in a class or at home? Read or listen.* 🎧

Vocabulary • Nouns for Talking About People

Look at the pictures. Say each word.

a teacher

a student

friends

neighbors

Comprehension: Confirming Content

Mark the following statements **true**, **false**, or **I don't know**.

		True	False	I don't know.
Example:	Amy and Bob are friends.	☑	☐	☐
1.	Amy and Bob are students.	☑	☐	☐
2.	This is an English class.	☐	☐	☑
3.	Bob is married.	☐	☐	☑
4.	Mary is a student.	☐	☑	☐
5.	Mary is an easy teacher.	☑	☐	☐

How to make informal introductions and talk about occupations

Verb Be: Use and Form		
statements		

I**'m** a teacher.　　　　　　　　　We**'re** in this class.
This *is* my friend Bob.　　　　　　Bill, Bob, and Jean *are* my friends.
He**'s** a student.　　　　　　　　　They**'re** all students.

subject pronoun	verb		contraction (short form)
singular			
I	*am*	⟶	I**'m**
you	*are*	⟶	you**'re**
he	*is*	⟶	he**'s**
she	*is*	⟶	she**'s**
it	*is*	⟶	it**'s**
plural			
we	*are*	⟶	we**'re**
you	*are*	⟶	you**'re**
they	*are*	⟶	they**'re**

GRAMMAR TASK: Find and circle all the subject pronouns in the photo story on pages 2–3.

Conversation 1

🎧 *Read and listen to the conversation.*

A: Hi. My name's Bill Blake.
B: Hi, Bill. Nice to meet you.
A: Nice to meet you, too.

🎧 *Listen again and practice.*

Pair Practice

Practice introductions with a partner. Learn your classmates' names.

A: Hi. My name's ___Elena___.

B: Hi, ___Elena___. Nice to meet you.

A: Nice to meet you, too.

Conversation 2

🎧 *Read and listen to the conversation.*

A: Sally, this is my friend Steve. Steve, this is Sally.
B: Hi, Sally. Nice to meet you.
C: Nice to meet you, too.

🎧 *Listen again and practice.*

Pair Practice

Practice introductions with two partners. Use their names.

A: _____, this is my friend _____. _____, this is _____.

B: Hi, _____. Nice to meet you.

C: Nice to meet you, too.

☑ **Now you know how to make informal introductions.**

Vocabulary • Occupations

🎧 *Look at the pictures. Say each word.*

a doctor

a homemaker

a lawyer

a nurse

a secretary

a student

a manager

an engineer

an artist

Conversation 3

🎧 *Read and listen to the conversation.*

A: Nice party.
B: Yeah, it's great.
A: So what do you do, Nadia?
B: I'm a nurse. What about you?
A: I'm an engineer.

🎧 *Listen again and practice.*

Pair Practice

Practice the conversation and vocabulary with a partner.
Use your own words.

A: Nice party.

B: Yeah, it's great.

A: So what do you do, _____?

B: I'm _____. What about you?

A: I'm _____.

☑ **Now you know how to talk about occupations.**

 **Look at the picture on page 13. Talk about the picture with a partner. Create a conversation. Use your own words.**

SOCIAL LANGUAGE AND GRAMMAR 2

HOW TO ask questions/make negative statements about people and things

Questions with Be	
yes-no questions	possible answers
Are you in this class?	Yes, I am.
Are you a student?	No, I'm not. I'm the teacher.
Is Mary a teacher?	Yes, she is.
Is the class hard?	No, it's not. (*or* No, it isn't.)
Am I late?	No, you're not.

TIP: Don't contract affirmative short answers: ***Yes, it is.*** (*not* ~~*Yes, it's.*~~)

wh- questions	possible answers
What's your name?	Katherine Baker.
Who's the teacher?	Mary Stanton.

GRAMMAR TASK: Answer the same two questions in your own words.

Negative Statements with Be
She'***s not*** the teacher. (*or* She ***isn't*** the teacher.)
I'***m not*** Bob.
We'***re not*** at home now. (*or* We ***aren't*** at home now.)

Grammar in a Context

Complete the conversation with the following words.

how's   I'm   is   Is   she's not   It's   What's
it is   It's   she's   am   Are   We're   is

 **In Your Own Words**

Look at the picture on page 13. Make true and false statements about the picture. Your partner corrects the false statements.

Reading

A Newspaper Article

Before You Read: Ask your teacher, "Where are you from?"

Read the newspaper article. 🎧

Comprehension: Factual Recall

Match the following words and phrases.

1. Mary Stanton ——— a state
2. Phillip Stanton ——— a city
3. Colorado ——— an instructor
4. Sacramento ——— an engineer
5. twenty-four ——— Mary's age
6. engineer ——— skiers
7. Mary and Phillip ——— Phillip's occupation

• Centerville Gazette •

Who's New?

We welcome Mary Stanton. Ms. Stanton is a new instructor here this year. "Centerville students are really interesting people," she says. "They're young and old, married and single. My classes are all interesting."

Mary and her husband, Phillip, are new to Colorado. They're from Sacramento, California. Phillip is an engineer for Dynamo Labs. Ms. Stanton says, "Colorado is wonderful! It's a great state, especially for skiers like Phil and me."

Mary is young. She's only twenty-four years old.

She says, "Sometimes students think I'm a student. They call me Mary. That's OK—if they're respectful. And sometimes they think I'm an easy teacher because I'm young. But they're wrong!" Welcome to Centerville, Ms. Mary Stanton!

SOCIAL LANGUAGE AND GRAMMAR 3

How to describe people

Indefinite and Definite Articles: A, An, The

Nouns are the names of persons, places, or things.

Use *a* or *an* with singular nouns.

singular noun | plural noun

Amy is **a student**. Amy and Bob are **students**.

Use *a* before a consonant sound.

a **t**eenager

Use *an* before a vowel sound.

an **adult**

Compare *a* and *the* in these examples.

Mary's *a* teacher.

Mary's *the* teacher.

Use *the* (not *a* or *an*) for specific persons or things.

a teenager / an adult

a student / a teacher

GRAMMAR TASK: Find and circle examples of *a* and *an* in the newspaper article about Mary. Then circle each noun that follows.

Vocabulary • Nouns and Adjectives That Describe People

Look at the pictures. Say each word.

a man / a woman

a teenager / an adult

a student / a teacher

athletic / studious

young / old

married / single

tall / short

In Your Own Words

Talk about the picture on page 13 with a partner. Examples: "He's short." "She's a teenager." Use your own words.

Heart to Heart

I think...
In my opinion...
because...

Circle the vocabulary words that describe you.

a man	a woman	a teenager	an adult
a student	a teacher	athletic	studious
married	single	young	old
tall	short		

Now, with a partner, ask and answer personal questions.

Examples: Are you athletic? Are you studious?
Are you married or single?
Are your classes hard?
Is your occupation interesting or boring?

I feel...
I don't think...
What about you?

Listening with a Purpose

Focus Attention

Read these words.

an animal	a human	married	single	Brazilian
American	real	fictional	old	young
athletic	studious	historical	a superhero	

🎧 *Look at the picture. Listen to the TV quiz program. Listen for the words.*

🎧 *Now listen again. Look at the words again and circle each word or phrase when you hear it.*

TIP: Circle only the words you hear. The other words are not on the tape.

Who Am I?

(reinforces describing people)

Work in pairs. One student selects a fictional or historical character. The other student guesses who it is.

Example: **A:** Are you a man?

B: Yes, I am, *etc.*

Then, with your partner, describe the character to the other pairs. They guess who it is.

Example: The character is a man / a woman.
He's / She's . . .

Pronunciation
The Alphabet

🎧 *Listen to the pronunciation of the letters.*

Capital letters

A B C D E F G H I J K L M N O P Q R S T U V W X Y Z

Lower-case letters

a b c d e f g h i j k l m n o p q r s t u v w x y z

🎧 *Listen again and repeat.*

🎧 *Now listen and write the names the speaker spells. Begin each name with a capital letter.*

1. _____   **3.** _____

2. _____   **4.** _____

Now spell your last name for a partner. Your partner writes your name here:

_____

Infocode

(reinforces meaning of first and last names)

Write your last name in code.

Example: Fox = 6 – 15 – 24   (F=6   O = 15   X = 24)

A	B	C	D	E	F	G	H	I	J	K	L	M
1	2	3	4	5	6	7	8	9	10	11	12	13

N	O	P	Q	R	S	T	U	V	W	X	Y	Z
14	15	16	17	18	19	20	21	22	23	24	25	26

_____

Your last name in code

Improvise

You know your classmates' first names. Circulate around the room.
Decode your classmates' last names. Then spell the names out loud.

Writing

Addressing an Envelope

Bruce is Bob's big brother. He is an English teacher in Chile.
Look at the envelope from Bruce's letter to Bob.

Bruce Mercer
Ecuador 261
Viña del Mar, Chile

> Bob Mercer
> 611 Elm Street
> Centerville, CO 80901
> U.S.A.

Correo Aéreo
Airmail

Complete the sentences in Bob's answer to his brother Bruce.
Use contractions when possible.

September 5

Dear Bruce,

Hi! Thanks for your letter. How'_____ Chile? ___Are___ you
very busy? How'_____ the skiing? Wow, skiing in September. Cool.

I have five classes this semester. __They are__ all good, and my
teachers __are__ all terrific, especially Mary Stanton. You don't
know her. __She is__ new. __She is__ great, and she's____ very
young. Her classes __are__ really interesting.

Well, _____ late for dinner. Write soon.

Bob

Now address the envelope to
Bruce. Use Bob's address as the
return address. Look at Bruce's
envelope as a model. Use capital
letters for names of people and
places. Use a comma (,) after
the city.

Warm up: Talk about this picture with a partner.
• Talk about the people. • What are their occupations?
• Ask your partner questions with **who.** • Describe the
people: young, old, teenager, etc. • What are they saying?

Then: Create conversations for the people. OR Tell a story
about the picture. Say as much as you can.

There's a noise downstairs!

Warm up: *Look at the pictures. Is it daytime or nighttime?*
Read or listen. 🎧

Hello?

Diana, this is Sandy.

Oh . . . Sandy. It's two o'clock in the morning! What's wrong?

Diana, I'm scared.

Scared? Why are you scared <u>this</u> time?

There's a noise downstairs. I'm sure there's someone in the house. I'm really scared.

Comprehension: Factual Recall

Circle the correct letter.

1. Who are Diana and Sandy?

   a. They're friends.   **b.** They're burglars.

2. Is there a burglar in Sandy's house?

   a. Yes, there is.   **b.** No, there isn't.

3. What is the problem in Sandy's house?

   a. There's a burglar.   **b.** There's a noise.

How TO **say the time**

Vocabulary • Telling Time

🎧 *Look at the pictures. Say each time.*

 2:00 = It's two o'clock.

 **2:07 = It's two-oh-seven.**

 **2:15 = It's two-fifteen**
or **a quarter after two.**

 **2:25 = It's two-twenty-five**
or **twenty-five after two.**

 **2:30 = It's two-thirty**
or **half past two.**

 **2:45 = It's two-forty-five**
or **a quarter to three.**

 **2:55 = It's two-fifty-five**
or **five to three.**

Receptive Model

Listening with a Purpose

Focus Attention

Look at this chart of theaters, movies, and times.

THEATER	MOVIE	SHOWTIME IN NUMBERS	SHOWTIME IN WORDS*
Theater 1	*My Favorite Vampire*		
Theater 1	*Invaders from the Underground*		
Theater 2	*Son of Dracula*		
Theater 2	*Elephant Woman*		

🎧 *Listen to the movie announcement.*

🎧 *Now listen again. Fill in the "showtime in numbers" column. Then write the showtime in words.*

* **Bonus Question**: Can you write each time in another way?

HOW TO **identify yourself on the phone/ask how someone is**

Conversation

🎧 *Read and listen to the conversation.*

A: Hello?
B: Carol, hi. This is Jennifer.
A: Oh hi, Jennifer. How are you?
B: Fine. I'm so excited.
A: Excited? Why?
B: *Elephant Woman* is at the Cineplex.
A: It is? That's great.

🎧 *Listen again and practice.*

Pair Practice

Practice the conversation with a partner.
Use your own words.

A: Hello?

B: _____, hi. This is _____.

A: Oh hi, _____. How are you?

B: Fine. I'm so excited.

A: Excited? Why?

B: _____ is at the Cineplex.

A: It is? That's great.

☑ **Now you know how to identify yourself on the telephone and ask how someone is.**

 **Look at the picture on page 25. Make true and false statements about the movies in the picture. Your partner corrects the false statements. Use your own words.**

How to **make plans to meet**

Conversation

🎧 *Read and listen to the conversation.*

A: There's a good movie at the Lido tonight.

B: What is it?

A: *Son of Dracula.* Do you want to go?

B: Maybe. What time?

A: Seven o'clock.

B: OK. See you there.

A: Terrific. See you later.

B: Bye.

🎧 *Listen again and practice.*

Pair Practice

Practice the conversation with a partner. Use this chart for ideas. Use your own words.

what? (events)			when?	what time?
a movie	a play	a concert	today tonight tomorrow	8:00 7:45 6:20

TIP: Use *at* for locations and for times: *There's a concert **at the theater at 8:00.***

A: There's a good _____ at the Lido _____.

B: What is it?

A: _____. Do you want to go?

B: Maybe. What time?

A: _____.

B: OK. See you there.

A: Terrific. See you later.

B: Bye.

☑ **Now you know how to make plans to meet.**

Vocabulary • Prepositions for Times of the Day and Dates

 *Look at the pictures. Say each phrase.*

in the **morning**   *in the* **afternoon**   *in the* **evening**   *on* **July fourth**

Improvise

Look at the schedule of events. Tell your partner about an event. Invite him or her to do something. Use this schedule of events and your own words and ideas.

Events This Week

Monday	Tuesday	Wednesday	Thursday	Friday	Saturday	Sunday
Guitar Concert Theater, 7:30 P.M.	Basketball Game Gym, 11 A.M.	Movie "War of the Worlds" Theater, 6:45 P.M.	Soccer Game Stadium, 3:30 P.M.	Rock Concert Theater, 8 P.M.	Play "Hamlet" Theater, 7 P.M.	Class Picnic Central Park, Noon

In Your Own Words

Look at the pictures on page 25. Talk about the pictures with a partner. What is the man saying? Use your own words.

HOW TO **describe things and places**

Count and Non-count Nouns: There Is / There Are

Nouns are the names of persons, places, or things.

A **count noun** is a noun you can count.

> one **book**, two **students**, ten **women**

Use **a** or **an** with a singular count noun.

> **a cat**

Use **there's (there is)** with a singular count noun.

> **There's a cat** in the house.

Use **there are** with a plural count noun.

> **There are two bedrooms** in this house.

A **non-count noun** is a noun that names a thing you cannot count.

> **music, air, information, bread, water**

Use **there's (there is)** with non-count nouns.

> **There's water** on the floor.

TIP: Do not use **a** or **an** before a non-count noun.

GRAMMAR TASK: Find and circle a sentence with **there is** or **there are** in "A Mystery Planet" on page 23.

Practice

Look at the pictures. Write the four count nouns together.
Write the four non-count nouns together.

water

bread

elephant

car

milk

orange

snow

dog

COUNT NOUNS **NON-COUNT NOUNS**

_____ _____ | _____ _____

_____ _____ | _____ _____

Grammar in a Context

*Welcome to Strange World. Find thirteen strange things in Strange World. Write **there is** or **there are** in the blanks. Use **a** or **an** if necessary.*

Everything is strange in Strange World. _____ two moons in the sky, and _____

ring around one of the moons. In this house, _____ car in the kitchen. _____

three telephones on the ceiling. _____ cat at the dining room table. _____ ice

in the kitchen, and _____ snow in the dining room. _____ bread in the glass,

and _____ water on the plate. _____ tree in the living room. _____

apples, oranges, and bananas on the tree. _____ elephant in the tree. _____

dog in the tree, too. Strange World is a very strange place.

   **Look at the room in the picture on page 25. With a partner, ask and answer questions about the room. Use *Is there* and *Are there*.**

Listening with a Purpose

Determine Context

🎧 *Listen to the conversation. Make notes on this chart.*

Who?	Where?	What?

🎧 *Now listen to the conversation again. Circle the correct letter.*

1. Who wants to buy something?

   a. the man   **b.** the woman

2. Where is the conversation taking place?

   a. in an airport   **b.** on the telephone

3. What is the subject of the conversation?

   a. seats for a flight   **b.** seats for a concert

Focus Attention

🎧 *Now listen again. Check the statement or question in each pair that you hear in the conversation.*

1. ☐ There are three flights today, sir.

    ☐ There are three flights every day, sir.

2. ☐ Yes, there are seats available, but only in the nonsmoking section.

    ☐ Yes, there are seats available, but only in the smoking section.

3. ☐ Well, is there a window seat available?

    ☐ Well, there is a window seat available.

4. ☐ What about my seat?

    ☐ What about an aisle seat?

5. ☐ That's great. I'll take it.

    ☐ That's great. We'll take it.

 ## Crazy Backwards Questions

*(reinforces questions with **be**)*

Partner B, turn to page 144.
Partner A, here is a list of five answers. Read each one to Partner B.
Partner B gives you a question for each answer.

Example: **A:** Three-thirty.
    B: What time is it?

1. **A:** Mary Stanton.
2. **A:** Eight-ten.
3. **A:** Yes, I am.
4. **A:** They're really boring.
5. **A:** At the Lido.

Partner A, now here is a list of five questions for Partner B's answers.

6. **A:** Is there a cat in this house?
7. **A:** How are you?
8. **A:** Is he married?
9. **A:** Who's that?
10. **A:** What's playing at the Cineplex?

Reading
Short Paragraphs

Before You Read: *Think about the names of all the planets you know.*
Read the paragraph and guess the mystery planet. 🎧

A Mystery Planet

Planet X is a very cold planet. There's ice here and maybe snow. It's also a very large planet. It's far from the sun—more than 1.4 billion kilometers. There are a lot of moons around Planet X—more than twenty. And there are rings around Planet X.

Is there life on Planet X? No one knows.

What planet is it? _____
ANSWER: SATURN

Comprehension: **Identifying the Main Idea**

*Choose another title for **A Mystery Planet.***

a. The Planet with Life   **b.** The Planet with Rings

Heart **to** **Heart**

I think...

In my opinion...   *because...*

Tell a partner about your favorite place. Make a list of reasons. Use **there is** and **there are.** Compare your list with a partner's list. Then make a class chart of favorite places and reasons.

I feel...   *I don't think...*

What about you?

▶ **W**riting

A Short Note to a Classmate

You want to go to the movies with a classmate tonight.

Look at the movie schedule on page 16. Invite your classmate with a short note.

Remember to use a capital letter for names of people, places, and titles. Remember to use a period at the end of sentences. Use a question mark (?) at the end of questions.

> **FROM THE DESK OF
> KEN TANAKA**
>
> *Hi, Monica:*
>
> *"My Favorite Vampire" is playing at the Lido today. There's a show at 4:45. Do you want to go?*
>
> *Ken*

▶ **P**ronunciation
/s/ , /z/ , /ɪz/

🎧 Listen to these plural nouns. Listen especially for the last sound in the word.

/s/	/z/	/ɪz/
elephants	animals	nurses
students	dogs	classes
cats	days	noises
flights	neighbors	places

🎧 Listen again and repeat.

🎧 Now listen to the words and write them in the correct columns.

ends in /s/	ends in /z/	ends in /ɪz/
_____	_____	_____
_____	_____	_____
_____	_____	_____
_____	_____	_____

Warm up: Talk about these pictures with a partner.
• Talk about the people. • What are they saying?
• Where are they? • What things are in the picture?
• Ask questions with **Is there** and **Are there**.

Then: Create conversations for the people. OR Tell a
story about the picture. Say as much as you can.

Unit 3

For computer questions, press one now.

Warm up: *Look at the pictures. Are the people at home or in an office? Read or listen.* 🎧

Comprehension: **Confirming Content**

*Mark the following statements **true**, **false**, or **I don't know**.*

	True	False	I don't know.
Example: Joanne and Frank have a fax machine.	☑	☐	☐
1. Their fax machine is broken.	☐	☐	☐
2. Joanne and Frank are at home.	☐	☐	☐
3. The representatives are all busy.	☐	☐	☐
4. Joanne is angry.	☐	☐	☐

HOW TO **suggest an activity/an alternative**

Commands and Suggestions with Let's		
affirmative commands	**negative commands**	**contraction**
Press five.	*Don't hang up.*	*don't* = do not
Be here at 6:00.	*Don't be* late.	
suggestions with *let's*		
Let's go to a movie.	*Let's not* watch a video.	

TIP: Use *please* with commands to be polite.

       Please press five.

       Please don't be late.

GRAMMAR TASK: Find and circle commands in the photo story on pages 26–27.

Conversation

🎧 *Read and listen to the conversation.*

A: Let's go to a movie tonight.

B: No, let's not go out. Let's watch a video instead.

A: Oh, all right. But I'm really hungry. Do you want to order a pizza?

B: OK. How about Mario's?

A: Good idea. Call Mario's.

🎧 *Listen again and practice.*

Vocabulary • Social Activities

🎧 *Look at the pictures. Say each phrase.*

go to a (rock) concert

go to a restaurant

go for a walk

go to a play

Pair Practice

Practice the conversation and vocabulary with a partner. Use your own words.

A: Let's _____ tonight.

B: No, let's not go out. Let's _____ instead.

A: Oh, all right. But I'm really hungry. Do you want to order a pizza?

B: OK. How about _____?

A: Good idea. Call _____.

☑ **Now you know how to suggest an activity and an alternative.**

 **Look at the picture on page 37. Create a conversation for the man and the woman. Use your own words.**

Pronunciation

Stress and Meaning

Look at how stress affects meaning:

Let's *call* them. (Let's not write them a letter.)

Let's call *them*. (Let's not call someone else.)

🎧 *Listen to the following pairs of sentences. Circle the word with the most stress.*

   a. Let's call them.

   b. Let's call them.

🎧 *Now listen again. Circle the letter of the correct explanation.*

1. Let's walk to the movies.

   a. Let's walk to the movies, not any other place.

   b. Let's walk to the movies, not drive.

2. Let's walk to the movies.

   a. Let's walk to the movies, not any other place.

   b. Let's walk to the movies, not drive.

Improvise

Make a list of five activities you like.

> **Examples:** playing sports, walking, going to the movies, etc.

Make suggestions to a partner to go somewhere. If you don't like an activity, say why not and suggest an alternative.

> **Example:** **A:** Let's walk on the beach.
>
> **B:** No, let's not. It's cold today.
>
> Let's _____ instead.

SOCIAL LANGUAGE AND GRAMMAR 2

How to state your address and telephone number

Possessive Adjectives and Possessive Nouns

My address is 75 Jones Street.

The *teacher's* phone number is 232-1748.

possessive adjectives

> my
> your
> his
> her
> its
> our
> their

TIP: Make subjects and possessive adjectives agree.

> *He* is in *his* room, and *she* is in *her* room.

possessive nouns

Use *'s* to make singular nouns possessive.

> My sister*'s* office is closed.
>
> Louis*'s* fax machine is broken.

Use an apostrophe (') to make a plural noun ending in *s* possessive.

> Her parent*s'* telephone number is 724-3636.

Use *'s* for plural nouns that don't end in *s*.

> The children*'s* cat is outside.

GRAMMAR TASK: Find and circle possessive adjectives in the photo story on pages 26–27.

Grammar in a Context

Complete the conversations with the correct possessive adjectives or possessive nouns.

1. Mom: Sally, where are you? _____ friends are here.
      <u>Their / Your</u>

   Sally: I'm up in _____ room, Mom.
      <u>my / its</u>

2. Dad: Let's go, kids. _____ flight is at 10:00.
      <u>Our / Its</u>

   Jessica: Jimmy's not ready, Dad. He's still in _____ room.
      <u>his / her</u>

3. Doctor's Office: Dr. _____ office. May I help you?
      <u>Stones / Stone's</u>

   Mr. Stanley: Yes, my daughter is sick. _____ temperature is 40 degrees.
      <u>Her / Your</u>

   Doctor's Office: You need to speak to Dr. Stone.

4. Dad: Is this a children's book?

   Mom: I think so. _____ title is *Goodnight Moon*.
      <u>Its / My</u>

5. Miranda: Is there a party at your _____ house?
      <u>grandparents' / grandparents</u>

   Paul: Yes, it's _____ 50th wedding anniversary.
      <u>your / their</u>

Conversation

🎧 *Read and listen to the conversation.*

A: This fax machine is broken.
B: No problem. Your name, please?
A: Joanne Tanaka.
B: Could you spell that, please?
A: Sure. T-A-N-A-K-A.
B: And your address?
A: 1640 Barkley Street.
B: Phone number?
A: 694-7021.
B: OK, Ms. Tanaka. I'll give you a call
when it's ready.

🎧 *Listen again and practice.*

Vocabulary • Machines and Appliances

🎧 *Look at the pictures. Say each word or phrase.*

a fax machine	a computer	a laptop	a remote

a TV	a CD player	a cassette player	a VCR

Pair Practice

Practice the conversation and vocabulary with a partner. Use your own words.

A: This _____ is broken.

B: No problem. Your name, please?

A: _____.

B: Could you spell that, please?

A: Sure. _____.

B: And your address?

A: _____.

B: Phone number?

A: _____.

B: OK, _____. I'll give you a call when it's ready.

☑ **Now you know how to give your address and telephone number.**

Look at the picture on page 37. Tell a partner the names of the machines in the living room.

How to **describe family relationships**

Vocabulary • Family Relationships

Look at the pictures. Say each word.

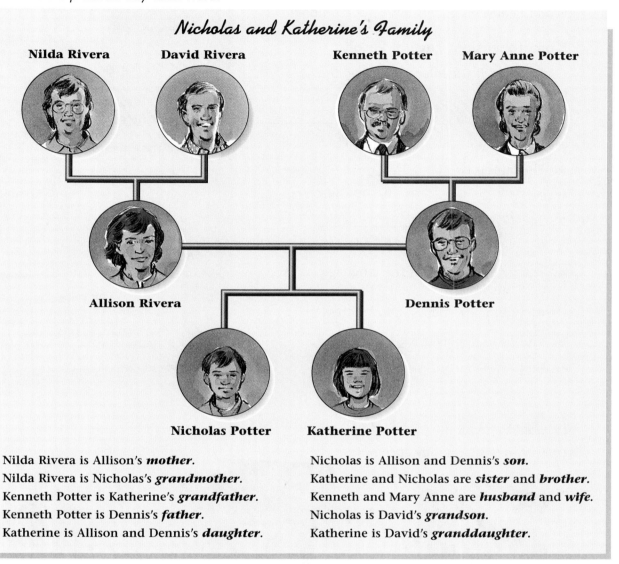

Nicholas and Katherine's Family

Nilda Rivera   **David Rivera**   **Kenneth Potter**   **Mary Anne Potter**

Allison Rivera   **Dennis Potter**

Nicholas Potter   **Katherine Potter**

Nilda Rivera is Allison's *mother*.
Nilda Rivera is Nicholas's *grandmother*.
Kenneth Potter is Katherine's *grandfather*.
Kenneth Potter is Dennis's *father*.
Katherine is Allison and Dennis's *daughter*.

Nicholas is Allison and Dennis's *son*.
Katherine and Nicholas are *sister* and *brother*.
Kenneth and Mary Anne are *husband* and *wife*.
Nicholas is David's *grandson*.
Katherine is David's *granddaughter*.

Grammar and Vocabulary with a Partner

Work with a partner. Write more sentences about this family and their relationships.
Then compare your sentences with other classmates' sentences.

Example: David is Nilda's husband.

   **Look at the picture on page 37. Find a photograph of this family.**
Talk about the people in the photograph.

Advertisements

Before You Read: Are there advertisements like these in your town or city?

Read the advertisements on the bulletin board. 🎧

Comprehension: Factual Recall

Complete each statement by circling the correct letter.

1. The car stereo cassette player is _____.
   a. new   **b.** Kim's

2. The laptop is _____.
   a. new   **b.** not new

3. 232-1776 is Jerome's _____.
   a. telephone number   **b.** address

4. The _____ of the language lab is 60 State Street.
   a. phone number   **b.** address

5. The cassette player is _____.
   a. Jerome's   **b.** Fred's

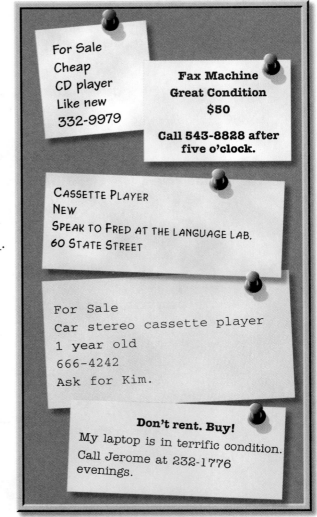

For Sale
Cheap
CD player
Like new
332-9979

**Fax Machine
Great Condition
$50**

**Call 543-8828 after
five o'clock.**

CASSETTE PLAYER
NEW
SPEAK TO FRED AT THE LANGUAGE LAB.
60 STATE STREET

For Sale
Car stereo cassette player
1 year old
666-4242
Ask for Kim.

Don't rent. Buy!
My laptop is in terrific condition.
Call Jerome at 232-1776
evenings.

Vocabulary • Classroom Commands

🎧 *Look at the pictures. Say each phrase.*

Stand up.

Go to the board.

Sit down.

Raise your hand.

Open your books.

Close your books.

 **"Please Do It"**

(reinforces commands)

Choose a leader.

Leader:

Give five commands from the vocabulary on page 34 to the class, one at a time.

Class:

Follow the leader's directions.

The Game:

Follow the leader's directions ONLY if the leader says "please."

Example: **Leader:** "Stand up, please."
or "Please stand up."
(Class stands up.)

Leader: "Stand up."
(Class *doesn't* stand up.)

Leader Bonus Points: *Use commands not on the vocabulary list on page 34.*

Class Bonus Points: *Help your classmates. Tell them, "Don't stand up!" if the leader doesn't say "please."*

Listening with a Purpose

Focus Attention 1

🎧 *Listen to the telephone voice mail message.*

leave	message	Jim	Jack
Toronto	Montreal	business group	tour group
Grandma	Grandpa	Billy	Alice
Nancy	Tuesday	Thursday	piano lesson
guitar lesson	brush their teeth	$1.65	$1.75

🎧 *Now listen to the telephone message again. Circle the words and phrases you hear.*

Focus Attention 2

🎧 *Now listen to some of the sentences again. Fill in the blanks.*

1. Please _____ a message after the tone.

2. To listen to _____ message, _____ one.

3. We're with _____ tour group this morning.

4. _____ forget to call Grandpa, OK?

5. And _____ sure they brush _____ teeth.

Writing
Phone Messages

🎧 *Listen to Joanne's voice mail. Leave her a message slip for each of her calls.*

Message	**Message**	**Message**
CALLER	CALLER	CALLER ....
FROM	FROM	FROM ....
PHONE NUMBER	PHONE NUMBER	PHONE NUMBER ....
MESSAGE	MESSAGE	MESSAGE ....
....	....	....

Heart to Heart

I think...   *In my opinion...*   *because...*

Look at the pictures. Which things are good or useful for you or your family?
Which things are not good or useful for you or your family? Why? Talk with a partner.
Compare your opinions.

I feel...   *I don't think...*   *What about you?*

Warm up: Talk about this picture with a partner.
• Ask questions about the picture. • Talk about the people.
• What are their relationships? • Where are they?
• What things are in the picture?

Then: Create conversations for the people. OR Tell a story about the picture. Say as much as you can.

Unit 4 — What's Bob doing?

Warm up: Look at the pictures. Where are these people?
Read or listen.

Luigi's Pizza. Great pizza. Great service. We deliver. This is Luigi.

A large pepperoni pizza. Extra cheese. Yes, sir.

Uh-huh. That's 2435 Meadow Lane. Phone 347-5235.

And you're Mr. Richards. Thank you. It's on its way.

George?

He's out. He's delivering a pizza.

What about Jim? Or Ted?

They're busy. They're serving customers.

Comprehension: Confirming Content

*Mark the following statements **true**, **false**, or **I don't know**.*

	True	False	I don't know.
Example: George is making pizzas.	☐	☑	☐
1. Bob is making pizzas.	☐	☐	☐
2. Luigi's is a restaurant.	☐	☐	☐
3. Mr. Richards is ordering pizza for lunch.	☐	☐	☐
4. Jim and Ted are out.	☐	☐	☐
5. Luigi is busy.	☐	☐	☐

HOW TO **talk about actions in progress/apologize/offer to call back later**

The Present Continuous

Use the present continuous to talk about actions in progress now.

> They**'re making** pizzas.

Form the present continuous with a form of **be** and a present participle.

> *be*   *present participle*
>
> Bob is working.

Make negative statements with **not**.

> I'm **not** working today.

Some statements in the present continuous describe activities over a period of time.

> *period of time in the present*
>
> We aren't driving to work this week.

TIP: How to use contractions in the present continuous:

> Bob**'s** working today.
>
> They **aren't** serving customers.

GRAMMAR TASK: Find sentences with the present continuous in the photo story on pages 38–39.

Conversation

🎧 *Read and listen to the conversation.*

A: Hello?

B: Hi, Sue. This is Ed. Are you busy?

A: Well, I'm making lunch right now. I'm sorry. Can I call you back?

B: Sure. No problem.

A: Bye.

🎧 *Listen again and practice.*

Vocabulary • Everyday Activities

🎧 *Look at the pictures. Say each word or phrase.*

exercise

make dinner

do homework

watch TV

talk to a friend

work

play ball

fix the car

Pair Practice

Practice the conversation and vocabulary with a partner. Use the vocabulary above and your own words.

A: Hello?

B: Hi, _____. This is _____. Are you busy?

A: Well, I'm _____ right now. I'm sorry. Can I call you back?

B: Sure. No problem.

A: Bye.

☑ **Now you know how to apologize and offer to call someone back when you are busy.**

The Present Continuous: Questions	
yes-no questions	**possible answers**
Are you doing your homework?	No, I'm not doing it now.
Is he making dinner?	Yes, he is.
TIP: Short answers to **yes-no** questions in the present continuous are the same as for **be**. Are you studying? **Yes, I am.**	
wh- questions	**possible answers**
Who's teaching this class?	Mr. Young is.
What are you doing?	Watching TV.
Where are you working?	In my room.
GRAMMAR TASK: Answer the same questions in your own words.	

Grammar and Vocabulary in a Context

Look at each picture. Complete the telephone conversations with forms of the present continuous.

Hi, Mandy. What _____?
1. you / do

_____ TV. It's a mystery story.
2. I / watch
It's really exciting. Can I call you back later?

Pete, is Luigi there?

I'm sorry, Mrs. Moreno. He's not here right now.

_____ a pizza?
6. he / deliver

I don't know where he is. Sorry.

Hi, Dad. How are the kids? _____?
3. they / sleep

No, honey. _____
4. They / play
outside with the other kids.

But Dad, it's nine-thirty in the evening!

Yes, but remember—there's no school tomorrow. _____ a good time. They're OK.
5. They / have

How's the weather there, Marsha? _____?
7. It / rain

No, _____ .
8. it / snow

Snowing? In April? That's too bad. It's beautiful here. _____.
9. The sun / shine

Grammar with a Partner

With a partner, write questions in the present continuous about the photo story on pages 38–39.

Example: Who's talking on the phone?

☑ **Now you know how to talk about actions in progress.**

Look at the picture on page 49. Make negative statements. (Example: "The girl is not talking on the telephone.")

Listening with a Purpose

Determine Context

🎧 *Listen to the telephone conversation. Make notes on this chart.*

Who?	What?	Where?

Now circle the correct letter.

1. Who is calling Luigi?

   a. Bob is.   **b.** George is.   **c.** Bob's dad is.

2. What is the problem?

   a. He's late.   **b.** He's scared.   **c.** He's busy.

3. Why?

   a. He's stuck in traffic.   **b.** He's busy.   **c.** He's studying.

4. How is he getting to the restaurant?

   a. He's driving.   **b.** He's walking.   **c.** He's delivering a pizza.

5. Where is he calling from?

   a. He's calling from his home phone.   **b.** He's calling from the pizzeria.   **c.** He's calling from a car.

SOCIAL LANGUAGE AND GRAMMAR 2

How to give directions to a place/talk about order

Conversation

🎧 *Read and listen to the conversation.*

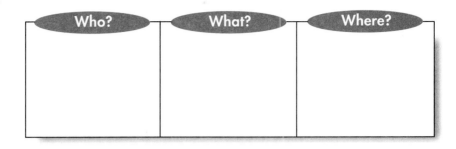

A: Hello?

B: Vicky, we're late. I'm sorry. We're lost.

A: Well, where are you calling from?

B: Uh, let's see. We're at the corner of Lincoln Avenue and Seventh Street.

A: OK. Go down Lincoln Avenue to the second light. Then turn left. We're the first house on the right. You can't miss it.

🎧 *Listen again and practice.*

Vocabulary • Ordinal Numbers 1–12

🎧 *Look at the pictures. Say each word.*

FIRST SECOND THIRD FOURTH FIFTH SIXTH SEVENTH EIGHTH NINTH TENTH ELEVENTH TWELFTH

Pair Practice

Practice the conversation and vocabulary with a partner. Use your own words.

A: Hello?

B: _____, _____ late. I'm sorry. _____ lost.

A: Well, where are you calling from?

B: Uh, let's see. We're at the corner of _____ and _____.

A: OK. Go down _____ to the _____. Then turn _____. We're the _____ house on the right. You can't miss it.

☑ **Now you know how to give directions to a place.**

Improvise

Look at the picture on page 49. Improvise a telephone conversation for the man and the woman. The woman apologizes. The man tells her what everyone in the room is doing.

Heart to Heart

I think... In my opinion... because...

With a partner, talk about lateness. Compare your opinions.

Are some people always late?

When a friend is late, is that OK?

I feel... I don't think... What about you?

Lost in Cascadia

(reinforces asking for and giving directions)

Look at this map of downtown Cascadia.
Work with a partner.

Partner B, look at page 144.

Partner A, you are lost in
Cascadia. You want to go to
one of these places:

Radio Shack
Farmers' Market
Cascadia Art Museum
Music Villa
Chong's Chinese Restaurant
Antoine's Fabulous French
     Restaurant
Pink Lotus Thai Restaurant
U.S. Post Office
Anita's Mexican Kitchen
Marvin's Department Store
Cineplex 12

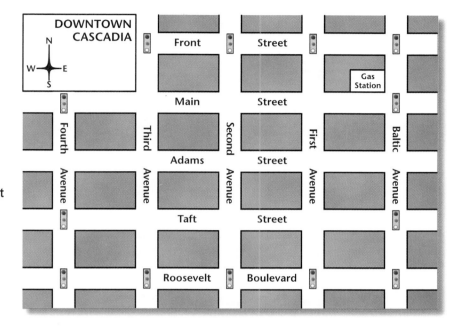

You stop at the gas station at the corner of Baltic Avenue and Main Street and use the
public phone. Your friend, Partner B, lives in Cascadia.

Call your friend and ask for directions. Then write the name of the place on your map.
Use the following locations and directions.

Vocabulary • Locations and Directions

🎧 *Read and listen to these sentences.*

Go down Main Street **to** Third Avenue.
It's **at the corner of** Main Street **and** Third Avenue.
Turn left.
Turn right.
It's **between** First Avenue **and** Second Avenue.

Example: **A:** Hello, _____? This is _____. I'm a little lost. I'm going
                  to the Farmers' Market. Right now I'm at a gas station at the
                  corner of Baltic Avenue and Main Street.

             B: No problem. Go down _____ to . . .

Switch roles and maps with Partner B. Now you give the directions.

HOW TO **talk about actions in progress (more practice)**

Read these sentences in the present continuous. Look at the subject and object pronouns.

subject pronoun   object pronoun

She's   calling   **him.**

subject pronoun   object pronoun

I'm   working with   **her**   at the restaurant.

object pronouns	
me	us
him	you
her	them
it	

GRAMMAR TASK: Look at the "First Day on the Job" conversation on page 47. Find and underline an object pronoun in it.

Grammar in a **C**ontext

Complete the conversations with the correct object pronouns.

1. Man: Jimmy, I'm fixing the car. Can you help _____?
                                                   1.

    Teenager: Sorry, I'm busy. But Sarah's not busy. Ask _____.
                                                               2.

2. First man: Is Adam waiting for you?

    Second man: Yes, I'm meeting _____ in front of the theater.
                                                     3.

3. Woman: Is that a good TV show?

    Young girl: Yes. Come and watch _____.
                                                    4.

4. Boy: Sue and I are playing Monopoly. Play with _____, Mom. Please?
                                                                   5.

    Woman: I'm busy. How about Dad and Will? Ask _____ to play with _____.
                                                   6.   **7.**

Reading

A Conversation with an Inventor

First Day on the Job

Before You Read: *Talk about this picture. Read the conversation.* 🎧

Dr. Dean is a professor and an inventor. Amy Lane is Dr. Dean's new assistant.

Dr. Dean: OK, Amy. Here's your desk. And this is your computer.

Amy: Oh, it's nice. Thanks. Wow! What's that on your lab table?

Dr. Dean: It's my invention. I'm still working on it.

Amy: Who are those people?

Dr. Dean: They're students. Right now you're looking at a history class. Look. The teacher is writing a date on the board.

Amy: Oh, it's a security system.

Dr. Dean: No, it isn't. And it's not electrical. It's similar to a crystal ball.

Amy: A crystal ball? You're kidding. That's magic.

Dr. Dean: No, Amy, it's not. It's real. Test it. Give me a name and a location.

Amy: How about Bob Mercer at Luigi's? He's working there right now.

Dr. Dean: Perfect. Look.

Amy: That's incredible. There he is. And he's making a pizza, too. Wow! What a fantastic invention!

Comprehension: Drawing Conclusions

*Mark the following statements **true** or **false**.*

	True	False
1. Amy is Dr. Dean's assistant.	☐	☐
2. Dr. Dean's invention is a security system.	☐	☐
3. Dr. Dean and Amy are in a history classroom.	☐	☐

What do you think? Is this story possible?

Writing

A Letter About What You Are Doing Now

Imagine you are a student with Dr. Dean's invention. It's nighttime. You are looking at someone or something right now.

Write a friend about it. In your letter, answer these questions about what you are watching: What is it? or Who is it? Where is the person or thing you are watching? What is that person doing? Where are you?

Remember to begin your letter with "Dear" and your friend's name. Use a comma. Put the month and the day at the top of the letter.

> May 26
>
> Dear Kevin,
>
>   Right now I'm sitting in my room. I'm using a wonderful new invention. It's fantastic. I'm watching the people in the pizzeria on the corner of Lexington Avenue and Third Street. Frank is making a pizza. He's talking to Anne. She's eating a pizza. This invention is not a camera. It's like magic. Incredible.
>
>   Talk to you soon.
>
>   Jane

Pronunciation

/iʸ/ and /ɪ/

🎧 *Listen to these words.*

/iʸ/	sleep	please	Dean	study	leave
/ɪ/	it	Jim	is	sit	live

🎧 *Listen again and repeat.*

🎧 *Listen to the words and place a check mark in the box of the sound you hear.*

> I'm **living** in an apartment on Baltic Avenue now.

> I'm **leaving** for work now. Talk to you later.

		/iʸ/	/ɪ/
1.	him	☐	☐
2.	teach	☐	☐
3.	isn't	☐	☐
4.	this	☐	☐
5.	she	☐	☐
6.	these	☐	☐
7.	pizza	☐	☐
8.	he	☐	☐
9.	cheese	☐	☐

Now read the words out loud.

Warm up: Talk about this picture with a partner. • Ask each other questions. • Talk about the people. • What are their relationships? • What time is it? • What is their address? • Where are these people? • Talk about what each person is doing. • Talk about the things and rooms in the house.

Then: Create conversations for the people. OR Tell a story about the picture. Say as much as you can.

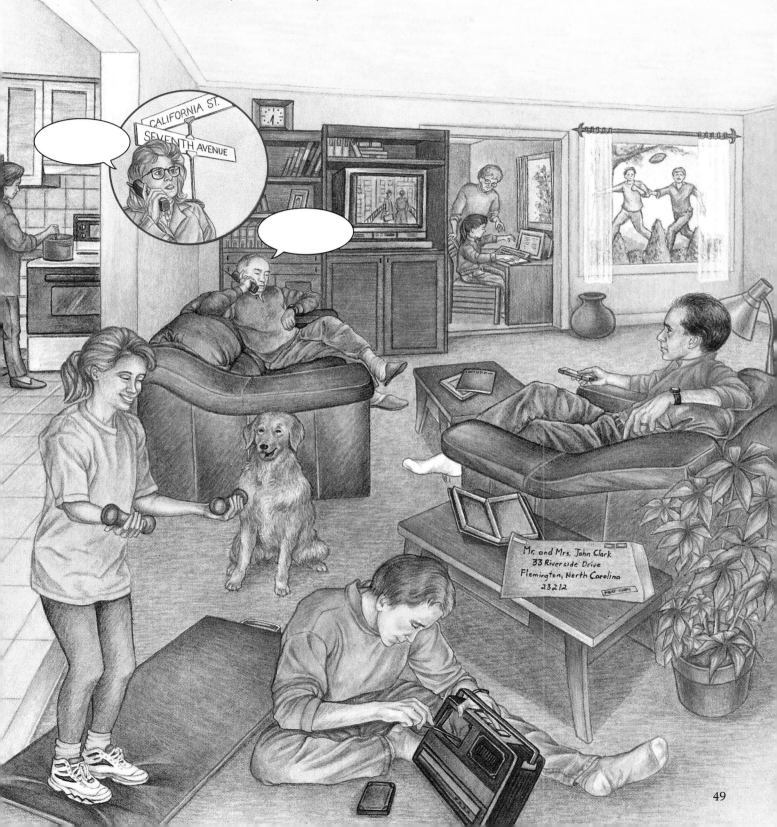

49

Receptive Model

Warm up: Look at the first picture. What are the partners' names?
Listen. 🎧

Doris Brand

Armstrong & Brand
Private Investigators

You lose it. — We find it.

Sam Armstrong

1

2

3

4

5

Percy Brand
1940-1988
Beloved
Husband
of Doris

Welcome to Computer class!

Comprehension: Confirming Content

*Now listen to "You lose it. We find It." again. Mark the following statements **true**, **false**, or **I don't know.***

	True	False	I don't know.
Example: Sam is a detective.	☑	☐	☐
1. Sam is married.	☐	☐	☐
2. Doris has children.	☐	☐	☐
3. Doris loves her work.	☐	☐	☐
4. Sam is a student.	☐	☐	☐
5. Doris works in two places.	☐	☐	☐

HOW TO **talk about work/ask about and express likes**

The Simple Present Tense

statements

Use the simple present tense to state facts and describe habitual actions.

> Many Americans **work** part-time. (fact)
>
> Judy **swims** three times a week. (habitual action)

In the simple present tense, use the base form of the verb with **I, you, we,** and **they**.

> I **work** part-time.

Use the base form + **-s** or **-es** with **he, she,** and **it.**

> Doris **works** part-time, too.

GRAMMAR TASK: Look at this sentence. Is it a habitual action or an action in progress?

> Sam is working at home tonight.

TIP: Remember to use the present continuous to talk about actions in progress now.

> What's Doris doing? She's **talking** to Sam.

yes-no questions	possible answers
Does he work with her?	Yes, he does.
Does she have a new computer?	No, she doesn't.
Sam, do I need a detective?	Yes, you do.
Do you work here?	Yes, I do.
Do they work with the detectives?	No, they don't.

GRAMMAR TASK: Find a *yes-no* question in the conversation below.

Conversation

🎧 *Read and listen to the conversation.*

A: Do you work?

B: Mm-hmm. I work part-time in a doctor's office— from three to five.

A: Oh. Do you like it?

B: Yes, I do. I like it a lot.

🎧 *Listen again and practice.*

Vocabulary • Places to Work

🎧 *Look at the pictures. Say each word.*

 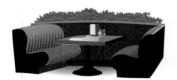  

a restaurant   **an office**   **a store**   **a supermarket**

Pair Practice

Practice the conversation and vocabulary with a partner. Use your own words.

A: Do you work?

B: Mm-hmm. I work part-time in _____—from _____.

A: Oh. Do you like it?

B: Yes, I do. I like it a lot.

☑ **Now you know how to talk about work and express likes.**

In Your Own Words — **Look at the picture on page 61. Ask a partner a *yes-no* question about the picture. Use *Do* or *Does* and your own words.**

SOCIAL LANGUAGE AND GRAMMAR 2

How To ask about studies/express dislikes

Vocabulary • Fields of Study

🎧 *Look at the pictures. Say each word.*

math   **art**   **medicine**   **music**   **dance**   **journalism**   **computers**   **business**

The Simple Present Tense	
wh- questions	possible answers
Who studies law?	Sam does.
What does Mary teach?	This class.
When do you go to class?	From ten to three.

Conversation

🎧 *Read and listen to the conversation.*

A: Do you study full-time?

B: No, I don't. I'm only taking two classes. What about you?

A: I study full-time at the university.

B: Oh. What do you study?

A: Drama.

B: Really? I bet that's fun. Do you like it?

A: No, not really.

🎧 *Listen again and practice.*

Vocabulary • Some Adjectives to Describe Studies

🎧 *Read and listen to these words.*

| interesting | easy | fun | exciting | boring | hard | difficult |

Pair Practice

Practice the conversation and vocabulary with a partner. Use your own words.

A: Do you study full-time?

B: No, I don't. I'm only taking _____. What about you?

A: _____.

B: Oh. What _____?

A: _____.

B: Really? I bet that's _____. Do you like it?

A: _____.

☑ **Now you know how to ask about studies. And you know how to say you don't like something.**

Look at the picture on page 61. With a partner, create a conversation for the tall man and the short woman. Use your own words.

Improvise

Work with a partner. Talk about your activities outside of class. Ask a lot of questions. Then tell the class about your partner. Say as much as you can.

Example: Do you work? Where do you work? etc.

Then: _____ works full-time. He likes his work.
He works in a bank, etc.

SOCIAL LANGUAGE AND GRAMMAR 3

How to talk about habitual activities (more practice)

Grammar in a Context

🎧 *Listen to these sentences about the detectives. Then complete them by choosing the verb you hear.*

1. Sam Armstrong _____ his work.
<u>loves / love</u>

2. He _____ missing people.
<u>finds / find</u>

3. He _____ information.
<u>gets / get</u>

4. Doris Brand _____ with Sam.
<u>works / work</u>

5. She _____ her partner.
<u>likes / like</u>

6. Sam and Doris _____ a detective agency.
<u>has / have</u>

7. Sam _____ law in the evenings.
<u>studies / study</u>

8. Doris _____ part-time.
<u>teach / teaches</u>

The Simple Present Tense: Spelling the Third-Person Form

If the base form ends in **sh, ch, x, s, z,** or **o,** add **-es:** tea**ch** / teach**es**

If the base form ends in a consonant plus **y,** change the **y** to **i** and add **-es:** worr**y** / worr**ies**

If the base form ends in any other letter, add **-s:** liv**e** / live**s**

TIP: The verb **have** is an exception: **have / has**

Reading

A Business Consultation with Detectives

Before You Read: Who are Sam and Doris? What is their occupation?

Read the conversation. 🎧

A Day in the Life of a Detective

Doris: OK, Mr. and Mrs. Mason. How can we help you?

Mrs. Mason: It's about our son Joe.

Sam: What about him? We're detectives. Is he missing or something?

Mrs. Mason: No, he's not missing. But some days he doesn't go to school.

Doris: Where's he spending the day?

Mr. Mason: That's what we want to know. Sometimes we follow him. But when we follow him, he always goes to school.

Mrs. Mason: Sometimes he goes to school every day for a month, but then he doesn't go for a day or two. We're worried.

Sam: Yes, you need a detective. It's impossible for you to follow him every day. That's a detective's job.

Doris: Do you have a recent picture of Joe?

Mrs. Mason: Yes, we do. Here it is.

Sam: How tall is he? What color is his hair? How old is he?

Mr. Mason: He has reddish curly hair. He's six feet tall. He's sixteen. And he always wears a green baseball cap.

Doris: What about his likes and dislikes?

Mrs. Mason: Well, he loves pizza . . . and fast food . . . and animals.

Comprehension: Identifying the Main Idea

Choose another title for "A Day in the Life of a Detective."

a. Joe Mason at School   **b.** A Problem for the Masons

Writing

A Detective's Notes

Sam and Doris keep notes of all their cases. Write notes on the Mason case for them.

Sam Armstrong • Doris Brand
Private Investigators

You lose it. We find it.

Case Notes

Case: Sophie Miller

Problem: Car is missing

Physical Description: Black 1998 Toyota

Other Information: She works at Acme Shoe Factory. She parks the car in the company parking lot every day.

Sam Armstrong • Doris Brand
Private Investigators

You lose it. We find it.

Case Notes

Case:

Problem:

Physical Description:

Other Information:

Receptive Model

Listening with a Purpose

Determine Context

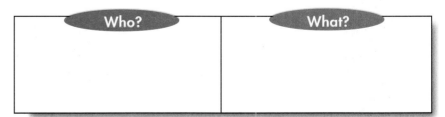

Who?	What?

🎧 *Listen to the conversation. Make notes on this chart as you listen.*

Circle the correct letter.

1. Who has a problem?

   a. Sam and Doris   **b.** Mr. and Mrs. Foley

2. The conversation is about _____.

   a. a missing person   **b.** a missing animal

Focus Attention

🎧 *Look at this picture. Listen to the conversation again. This time, listen specifically for names. Then write the name of each person and animal you hear about in the conversation.*

SOCIAL LANGUAGE AND GRAMMAR 4

HOW TO **talk about likes and dislikes/describe habitual activities (more practice)**

The Simple Present Tense: Negative

Form the negative of **I, we, you,** and **they** with **don't** + the base form of the verb.

    I **don't like** pizza, but I love cheese.

Form the negative of **he, she,** and **it** with **doesn't** + the base form of the verb.

    Doris **doesn't have** a son.

TIP: The uncontracted forms (**do not** and **does not**) make negative statements stronger.

GRAMMAR TASK: Find and underline sentences with negative forms of the simple present tense in the reading on page 56.

Look at the picture on page 61. With a partner, write as many sentences in your own words as you can about this picture in one minute. Which pair of students writes the most sentences?

Be a Detective

(reinforces questions in the simple present tense)

Walk around your classroom for three minutes. Find people who fit these categories. Ask questions. Get each person's initials.

Example:　Do you eat breakfast?

POINTS FOR EACH THING	FIND SOMEONE WHO	PERSON'S INITIALS	YOUR SCORE
2	doesn't eat breakfast	J.S.	2
2	hates spiders	L.M.	4
4	doesn't live in a house		
8	speaks German		
10	likes to eat snails		
1	eats at fast-food restaurants		
7	doesn't like rock music		
10	likes snakes		
6	has an unusual pet (not a cat or dog)		
8	hates sports		
3	wears contact lenses		
8	doesn't like fast food		
9	studies ballet		
7	likes opera		
5	worries a lot		
6	has a coin with a date before 1990		
8	doesn't drink coffee		
9	doesn't eat meat		

your total score _____

Use the chart and talk about your classmates' likes and dislikes.

Heart to Heart

Compare your likes and dislikes with a partner's. Compare your favorite things.

Talk about these categories.

TV programs	kinds of music	places
activities	foods	kinds of people

I think... *In my opinion...* *because...* *I feel...* *I don't think...* *What about you?*

Pronunciation

/s/, /z/, /ɪz/

🎧 Read and listen to the following verbs.

ends in an /s/ sound		**ends in a /z/ sound**		**ends in an /ɪz/ sound**	
write	writes	run	runs	wash	washes
make	makes	love	loves	watch	watches
like	likes	study	studies	teach	teaches

🎧 Listen again and repeat.

🎧 Now listen to the following verbs and write them in the correct columns, according to the sound you hear.

ends in an /s/ sound	**ends in a /z/ sound**	**ends in an /ɪz/ sound**
_____	_____	_____
_____	_____	_____
_____	_____	_____
_____	_____	_____

Warm up: Talk about this picture with a partner.
• Where is this? • Talk about the people in the picture.
• What are they doing? • What are they saying?
• Who is at the window? • What do you see in the picture?

Then: Create conversations for the people. OR Tell a story about the picture. Say as much as you can.

Review, SelfTest, and Extra Practice

Part 1

Review

Computer Class

🎧 *Read or listen to this conversation in a computer class.*

Doris Brand is the teacher. Steve and Alice are her students.

Doris: Hi, everybody. Welcome back. Ready? OK. Here we go. Please turn on your computers first. OK. Now is everyone in File Manager?

Steve: Uh-oh. This is really different! All my training is on the Mac.

Alice: Don't worry. It's not that hard.

Steve: Are you pretty advanced at this stuff?

Alice: Not really. Photography is my hobby, so I'm here to learn computer graphics.

Doris: Steve, do you need help?

Steve: Well . . . yes, I do. I'm new to the PC, and I'm not a computer genius.

Doris: Just treat it like the Mac. It's pretty similar.

Alice: Really. Don't worry. Let's talk after class.

Steve: Great. Thanks.

Comprehension: Confirming Content

🎧 *Read or listen again to the conversation in Doris's computer class.*
*Then mark the following statements **true, false,** or **I don't know.***

		True	False	I don't know.
Example:	Doris's class is an English class.	☐	☑	☐
1.	Doris teaches a computer class.	☐	☐	☐
2.	Steve has a Mac at home.	☐	☐	☐
3.	Alice wants to learn computer graphics.	☐	☐	☐
4.	Alice is married.	☐	☐	☐
5.	Steve is a computer genius.	☐	☐	☐

Improvise

With a partner, pretend you are students in a computer class
(or another kind of class: art, cooking, photography, etc.).
One student is worried. The other student wants to help.
Have a conversation.

Extra Practice

Part 2

Review

An Invitation

🎧 *Listen to Steve and Alice's*
conversation after class.

Grammar: Verb Review

🎧 *Listen again to Steve and Alice's conversation after class. Fill in the blanks with the correct pronouns and verb forms. Remember to use a capital letter if a word begins a sentence.*

Alice: Well, Steve. _____ me about yourself. What do you do?
                              1.

Steve: Well, _____ see. _____ a student here at the college.
                     2.   **3.**

Uh . . . I _____ soccer for the college, too.
            4.

Alice: Soccer? _____ great. I _____ soccer. And what _____ you _____?
                      5.   **6.**   **7.**   **8.**

Steve: Physical education. I _____ sports.
                                  9.

Alice: _____ you _____ with friends?
            10.   **11.**

Steve: Uh, no, I _____. I _____ alone.
                      12.   **13.**

Alice: _____ you _____ the college?
            14.   **15.**

Steve: Well, _____ OK. But my business classes _____ really
                  16.   **17.**

hard. I have to work with spreadsheets and data bases. I really

_____ about that. And now this class _____ a different computer.
  18.   **19.**

Alice: I _____ an idea. Why _____ you _____ to my house
            20.   **21.**   **22.**

tomorrow and meet my grandson? _____ a computer whiz.
                                  23.

Steve: Oh . . . no, I . . . uh . . . have to study.

Alice: Oh come on. Tomorrow night at seven-thirty? 610 13th Avenue.

Steve: _____ you sure?
            24.

Alice: Of course. See you tomorrow evening.

Steve: Thanks a lot.

Pair Practice

Talk with a partner about work and studies. Use this conversation as a guide.

A: Do you _____? (work/study)

B: _____.

A: I bet that's _____.

B: _____. What about you?

A: _____.

B: Do you like it?

A: _____.

Part 3

Review

New Friends

Read or listen to the conversation at Alice's house the next day.

SelfTest

Comprehension: Factual Recall

Circle the correct letter.

1. Who is Charlie?

   a. Steve's friend   **b.** Alice's grandson   **c.** Julie's grandson

2. Who is Julie?

   a. Alice's granddaughter   **b.** Steve's friend   **c.** Charlie's friend

3. Where are these people talking to each other?

   a. in Doris's computer class   **b.** in Alice's house   **c.** at the college

4. What does Charlie love?

   a. computers   **b.** the college   **c.** physical education

5. What does Julie study at the college?

   a. French   **b.** physical education   **c.** computers

Extra Practice

Improvise

Work with a partner. Review the conversations on pages 62 and 64. Then improvise a similar conversation, asking each other about activities outside of class. Finish by inviting your partner to do something with you or suggesting some place to go.

Part 4

Review

Vocabulary: Parts of the Computer

the printer

the screen

an icon

the mouse

the keyboard

Space Invaders

🎧 *First look at the computer vocabulary above. Then read or listen to Steve and Charlie's conversation after dinner.*

Charlie: I've got a great idea. Let's play a game on my PC. Maybe it sounds silly, but it's a great way for you to learn the PC.

Steve: What about Space Invaders? I know that one. My little sister plays it all the time. Do you have that?

Charlie: Hmm. Yeah, I do. . . . OK, Steve. You're in the driver's seat. You take the mouse.

Steve: OK. Here we go.

Charlie: All right. Now select that icon.

Steve: Cool. That's Zorgon. How do I select it?

Charlie: The same as on the Mac. Click on it.

Steve: OK. What's next?

Charlie: Simple. You zap the invaders. Like this.

Steve: My sister isn't going to believe this—her big brother playing Space Invaders.

Charlie: Steve, watch out! There are the invaders! Oh no! Too late. Zorgon's dead.

Steve: Oh well. Too bad. Maybe next time. Want to play again?

Grammar: Definite and Indefinite Articles: *a, an, the*

*Read the conversation about Space Invaders on page 67. Use the information in that conversation to complete this paragraph with **a, an, the,** or no article.*

Steve and Charlie are in Charlie's room, playing _____ computer games.
1.

Space Invaders is _____ computer game. It's _____ fun. When you play
2. **3.**

Space Invaders, you click on _____ zoom box to maximize _____ screen.
4. **5.**

Zorgon is _____ hero. He fights with _____ invaders. Sometimes
6. **7.**

_____ invaders win. Sometimes _____ Zorgon wins.
8. **9.**

Writing
Describing a Game

Describe Space Invaders or your favorite computer game. Use the conversation on page 67 as a model.

Extra Practice

Part 5

Review

Technology in Our Lives

Are you afraid of technology? Is technology a good thing? Many Americans think so. In the United States, about 90 percent of families have television. About 99 percent of the 90 percent have color TV. About 79 percent have a VCR. Almost 40 percent have a computer. Many people have CD players. Many people have a vacuum cleaner, a washing machine, and a dryer.

But not everyone loves technology. Mrs. Amanda Titus of Dallas, Texas, doesn't like it at all. She says, "I hate modern inventions. They control our lives. I have a remote for my TV, and I don't know how to use it. My daughter watches TV all the time. She doesn't talk to me. My son plays computer games constantly. He doesn't do his homework. I'm afraid of technology. It controls our lives."

What do you think?

Reading Comprehension: Factual Recall

Complete the answers to items 1, 2, and 3. Then provide reasons for item 4.

1. _____ percent of American homes have television.

2. _____ percent of American homes have a VCR.

3. Many Americans have _____, _____, and _____.

4. What are three reasons Mrs. Amanda Titus doesn't like technology?

   a. _____

   b. _____

   c. _____

I think...

In my opinion... *because...*

I feel...

Extra Practice

Talk to a partner. Compare your opinions. Do you agree or disagree with Amanda Titus? Give examples and reasons for your opinions.

I don't think...

What about you?

SOCIAL **LANGUAGE** SelfTest

Circle the appropriate statement or question to complete each of the following conversations.

1. A: I'm Jeanette Young.

  B: _____

    a. Hi, I'm Susan Peters. Nice to meet you.   **c.** Nice to meet you, too.

    b. Yes, I am.   **d.** What's your name?

2. A: _____

  B: It's nice to meet you, too.

    a. What's your name?   **c.** I'm a nice teacher.

    b. It's nice to meet you.   **d.** She's a teacher.

3. A: What's his name?

   B: _____

      a. Bob Stettner.   **c.** My name's Mark Smith.

      b. Amy Carlson.   **d.** Who's he?

4. A: There's a great movie at the Lido.

   B: _____

      a. Really?   **c.** Seven o'clock.

      b. How are you?   **d.** Who's that?

5. A: See you there.

   B: _____

      a. What is it?   **c.** OK.

      b. Why?   **d.** There's a rock concert at the stadium.

6. A: Do you want to go?

   B: _____

      a. See you later.   **c.** Bye.

      b. I'm so excited.   **d.** Maybe. What time?

7. A: What's your name and address?

   B: _____

      a. Michael Harris. 33 Riverside Drive.   **c.** 238-5803.

      b. China King Restaurant.   **d.** Anything else?

8. A: _____

   B: No, let's not. I'm tired.

      a. How's it going?   **c.** Call Mario's. Their pizza's great.

      b. Don't hang up.   **d.** Do you want to go to the movies tonight?

9. A: Spell your last name, please.

   B: _____

   a. 238-5803.   c. Frances Silva.

   b. A-M-E-S.   d. Don't worry.

10. A: What number are you calling from?

   B: _____

   a. Nice to meet you, too.   c. 422-6701.

   b. My son is very sick.   d. 1214 Elm Street.

11. A: _____

   B: My homework.

   a. Where are you calling from?   c. What are you doing?

   b. Do you work here?   d. Who's that?

12. A: Do you work?

   B: _____

   a. I like it a lot.   c. He works from 10 to 3.

   b. No, I don't.   d. In a doctor's office.

13. A: Do you like your job?

   B: _____

   a. I work part-time.   c. He doesn't have a job.

   b. I study full-ime.   d. Yes, I do.

14. A: I bet that's hard.

   B: _____

   a. Do you like it?   c. No, I don't.

   b. How are you?   d. Not really.

Unit 6

We're going to win.

Warm up: *Look at the young man. Is he happy or unhappy?*
Read or listen. 🎧

Great game, guys. Thanks to you, we're going to win the College Cup.

Steve? What's wrong? You look miserable. Are you OK?

Well. . . I never have a date after the game.

You don't? Why not? Girls love athletes.

Well, yeah. But they don't love me.

Comprehension: Drawing Conclusions

*Mark the following statements **true** or **false**.*

	True	False
1. Steve and the coach are talking before the game.	☐	☐
2. Steve is an athlete.	☐	☐
3. The coach is interested in his players' problems.	☐	☐
4. Steve never talks about his problems.	☐	☐

HOW TO **ask for an appointment/talk about aches and pains**

Conversation

🎧 *Read and listen to the conversation.*

A: Springfield Medical Group.
B: Hello. This is Peter Tanaka
I'm Dr. Taylor's patient.
A: Yes, Mr. Tanaka. How can I help you?
B: I need an appointment. My right knee
hurts.

🎧 *Listen again and practice.*

Vocabulary • Parts of the Body

🎧 *Look at the picture. Say each word.*

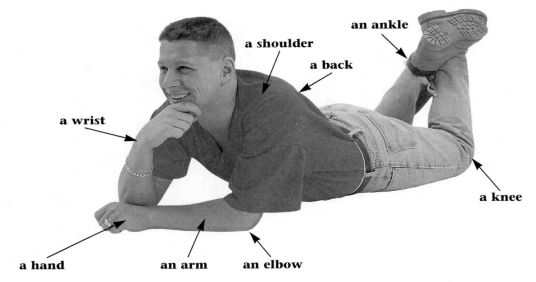

a shoulder
a back
an ankle
a wrist
a knee
a hand
an arm
an elbow

Pair Practice

Practice the conversation and vocabulary with a partner. Use your own words.

A: Springfield Medical Group.

B: Hello. This is _____. I'm Dr. _____'s patient.

A: Yes, _____. How can I help you?

B: I need an appointment. My _____ hurts.

☑ **Now you know how to ask for an appointment and talk about aches and pains.**

HOW TO **describe plans/make an appointment/talk about illnesses**

The Future with Be Going To

One way to express the future is to use a form of *be (am / is / are)* + *going to* + the base form of a verb.

| | be | going to | base form |

I can't go to the meeting tomorrow. I**'m** *going to* *be* with my family.

wh- questions	possible answers
What are you going to do tonight?	Nothing. I'm going to stay home.
What is Steve going to do tomorrow?	He's going to play soccer.

GRAMMAR TASK: Answer one of the questions in your own words.

Grammar in a Context

*Complete each sentence with a form of **be going to** and the indicated verb. Use contractions with pronouns.*

Hi, honey. Don't wait for me.
_____ late.
1. I / be

Steve _____ a
2. make
phone call.

Judy and her dog Fluffy
_____ a walk.
3. take

Kids, come on in! _____.
4. It / rain

In Your Own Words

Look at the picture on page 83. Create a conversation for the two women with the newspaper. Use your own words.

Conversation

🎧 *Read and listen to the conversation.*

B: I need to see Dr. Taylor.

A: How about three-fifteen this afternoon?

B: This afternoon? Gosh, I'm going to be in a meeting until five. Is tomorrow a possibility?

A: Let's see. . . . How about ten-thirty tomorrow morning?

B: Ten-thirty tomorrow? Yes. That's fine. Thank you.

A: You're welcome. See you then. Good-bye.

B: Bye.

🎧 *Listen again and practice.*

Vocabulary • General Locations

🎧 *Say each phrase.*

at work	*at* school	*at* home	*in* class	*out of* town	*in the* city

Pair Practice

Practice the conversation and vocabulary with a partner. Use your own words.

B: I need to see Dr. _____.

A: How about _____ this afternoon?

B: This afternoon? Gosh, I'm going to be _____ until _____.

Is tomorrow a possibility?

A: Let's see. . . . How about _____?

B: _____? Yes. That's fine. Thank you.

A: You're welcome. See you then. Good-bye.

B: Bye.

☑ **Now you know how to make an appointment.**

Vocabulary • Aches, Pains, and Illnesses

 *Look at the pictures. Say each phrase.*

have a sore throat   **have a fever**   **have a toothache**   **be dizzy**

have a cough   **have a headache**   **have a backache**

 **In Your Own Words**

Look at the picture on page 83. With a partner, create a telephone conversation for the receptionist and the woman. Use your own words.

Improvise

Working with a partner, make an appointment to visit your doctor or dentist. Look at the vocabulary above for examples of some physical problems. Say as much as you can.

SOCIAL LANGUAGE AND GRAMMAR 3

HOW TO **talk about frequency/describe feelings**

Vocabulary • Words That Tell How Often Something Happens

 Look at the chart. Say each frequency adverb.

never	occasionally	sometimes	often	usually	always
	seldom				
	rarely				

(0% of the time ⟵——————————⟶ 100% of the time)

Placement of Frequency Adverbs

Look at this sentence with **be**.

> Steve is **never** nervous before a game.

Where is the frequency adverb? Is it before or after the verb?

Now look at this sentence in the simple present tense.

> Steve's coach **always** has time for his players.

Where is the frequency adverb? Is it before or after the verb?

In sentences in the simple present tense, place frequency adverbs before the verb.
In sentences with **be,** place frequency adverbs after the verb.

TIP: *Sometimes, occasionally*, and *usually* can go at the beginning of a sentence, too.

> *Sometimes* the coach helps the players with their problems.

GRAMMAR TASK: Find a frequency adverb in the photo story on pages 72–73.

Grammar with a Partner

First, write five sentences with the cues below. Use a frequency adverb in each sentence.
Exchange sentences with a partner. Then, tell another person about your partner.

1. I / be / worried / before a test. _____

2. I / be / excited / before a date. _____

3. I / feel / nervous / in front of the class. _____

4. I / feel / tired / after work. _____

5. I / be / bored / in meetings. _____

☑ **Now you know how to talk about frequency.**

Listening with a Purpose

Receptive Model

Determine Context

🎧 *Listen to the conversation. Make notes on this chart.*
Then complete each sentence by circling the correct letter.

Who?	What?

1. This is _____.

    a. a TV show   **b.** a telephone conversation   **c.** a radio show

2. The conversation is an interview of _____.

    a. a coach   **b.** a politician   **c.** a student

3. An important subject of the interview is _____.

    a. the coach's children   **b.** the coach's house   **c.** the coach's work

Focus Attention

🎧 *Read the following sentences. Then listen to the interview again and complete the sentences by circling the correct letter.*

1. The name of the coach is _____.

  a. Walter Anderson **b.** Charlotte Matthews

2. The name of the program is _____.

  a. *Everybody's Favorite Coach* **b.** *People on Campus*

3. The coach's teams are baseball, volleyball, and _____.

  a. tennis **b.** soccer

4. _____ is married.

  a. The coach **b.** The boy

5. _____ like to watch TV.

  a. The Andersons **b.** The Matthews

6. _____ has no children.

  a. Ms. Matthews **b.** Mr. Anderson

7. _____ is trying to help a boy.

  a. Charlotte **b.** Walter

8. The name of the radio station is _____.

  a. Trinity College Radio **b.** Charlotte Matthews

Receptive Model

Reading
A Magazine Advice Column

Before You Read: *Dr. Naomi Brown is a psychologist. She writes an advice column in a magazine. Do you like advice columns?*

Read the column. 🎧

Dear Dr. Naomi,

My husband is driving me crazy. He gets up at five o'clock, come rain or shine. Then he exercises until seven. He's a coach. He eats, breathes, and sleeps sports.

He has a soccer team, a baseball team, and a women's volleyball team. He works with them every day, even on holidays. At four-thirty he comes home. Of course he's always tired, so we never go out. From four-thirty until nine o'clock (when he goes to bed), he watches TV. Then what does he watch? Sports. Sports. Always.

I hate sports. Sports are ruining my life. I really don't know what I'm going to do. I need your help.

A Sports Widow in the Midwest

Writing

A Business Letter

Steve Costa reads the Sports Widow's letter in Dr. Brown's column. He thinks her husband is Coach Anderson. He wants to write to Dr. Brown about his wonderful coach.

🎧 *Listen to Coach Anderson's interview again for information.*

Pretend you are Steve. Write about Coach Anderson to the Sports Widow. Tell her why he is important to you. Use some of these words in your letter.

> **help   always   when   problem   game**
> **date   computer dating service**

Use the example as a model for writing the date and address.

Dr. Naomi Brown's Column
Truly Yours Magazine
1416 Broadway
New York, NY 10018

July 21

Re: My answer to "Sports Widow in the Midwest"

Dear Sports Widow,

I have a wonderful coach. His name is Walter Anderson. He is

Sports Marathon

*(reinforces **wh**- questions and answers)*

Play in pairs or small teams. Use two coins as place markers. Take turns. Toss another coin to move. One side of the coin lets you move one space. The other side lets you move two. Answer the questions. If your answer is correct, take another turn.

1 START	**2**	**3** Who is the coach of your national soccer team?	**4** How many players are there on a basketball team?	**5**
10 Name a famous figure skater.	**9** Name two professional baseball teams.	**8** How many players are there in a doubles match?	**7**	**6** Name two famous women who are gymnasts.
11	**12** Name two stadiums.	**13**	**14** Name three Olympic sports.	**15** How many rounds are there in a championship boxing match?
20 FINISH LINE	**19**	**18** Name a Formula 1 Grand Prix champion.	**17** What team is a four-time World Cup winner?	**16**

Reading
A Computer Dating Interview

Before You Read: Talk about Steve. Why is he going to a computer dating service?

Read the interview. 🎧

The Interview

Interviewer: Great Date Computer Dating Service. Interview 552. Today we're going to interview Steve Costa. Ready, Steve?

Steve: Ready.

Interviewer: Good. How old are you?

Steve: I'm twenty.

Interviewer: OK. What do you do, Steve?

Steve: I'm a student at Trinity College. I'm working on a degree in physical education.

Interviewer: Great, Steve. You're an athlete, then?

Steve: Yes. I play soccer on the college team.

Interviewer: Other interests? Hobbies, movies, music? What do you like to do?

Steve: Well, sports are really my only hobby. I practice soccer every day, and I watch sports on TV. Movies? I think action movies are great. I go to the movies almost every Saturday. But I usually go with my teammates.

Interviewer: Fine. Anything else? Music?

Steve: I enjoy pop, and I love Brazilian music. I listen to it on the radio, but I don't go to concerts very often.

Interviewer: OK. Now, what don't you like?

Steve: Ugh . . . weird food. And opera. And . . . let me think . . . complicated computer software.

Interviewer: Don't worry. Thanks, Steve. Let's see if <u>our</u> computer can find you someone special.

Comprehension: Interpretation and Analysis

You are thinking of a place to invite Steve. Which of these activities is Steve going to prefer?

a. watching a tennis match   **b.** going to the opera

Listening with a Purpose

Focus Attention

🎧 *Look at this chart. Study the first column. Then listen for the information you need to complete the chart.*

Read Steve's interview again on page 81. Whose name is Great Date Computer Dating Service going to give Steve?

	Interview 1	Interview 2
Name	Julie	
Age		24
Occupation		
Favorite Music	pop	
Likes		
Dislikes		sports

Heart to Heart

I think...

In my opinion...

because...

Talk to a partner about dating and meeting people. Compare your opinions.

Do you think Steve and Julie are going to like each other?

What do you think about computer dating services?

Are they good?

I feel...

I don't think...

What about you?

Pronunciation

Intonation of Questions

🎧 *Listen to these questions. Notice the different intonations. Are they rising ↑ or falling ↓?*

> What are you doing?   Are you a doctor?   How can I help you?   Do you want aspirin?

🎧 *Listen to the questions again and repeat them.*

🎧 *Listen to these questions. Check the intonation you hear.*

	Rising ↑	Falling ↓
1. Where do you live?	☐	☐
2. Is this your textbook?	☐	☐
3. How are you?	☐	☐
4. Do you like baseball?	☐	☐

TIPS: *Yes-no* questions have an intonation pattern that rises at the end.

Wh- questions have an intonation pattern that falls at the end.

Warm up: Talk about this picture with a partner. • What is each person doing? • Where are the people? • What things are in the picture?

Then: Talk with a partner about Dr. Harris. What is he going to do the next day? Talk about the people in the picture. Describe the room. Say as much as you can. OR Create conversations for the people.

83

Can you dance?

Warm up: Look at the photos. What are the two people talking about? Read or listen. 🎧

Comprehension: Confirming Content

*Mark the following statements **true**, **false**, or **I don't know**.*

		True	False	I don't know.
Example:	Margaret and Richard are dance partners in the talent show.	☑	☐	☐
1.	Richard and Margaret work at the same company.	☐	☐	☐
2.	Richard is Margaret's boss.	☐	☐	☐
3.	Margaret thinks she can't dance.	☐	☐	☐
4.	Richard likes dancing.	☐	☐	☐
5.	Richard wants to go dancing tonight.	☐	☐	☐
6.	Margaret is in love with Richard.	☐	☐	☐

How TO **express obligations and regrets**

Have to / Has to **for Obligation**

To express an obligation, use **have to** or **has to** plus the base form of a verb.

base form

I **have to study** tonight. I have a test tomorrow.

Use **has to** plus the base form in the third-person singular.

base form

Margaret **has to work** tonight.

Remember that **have** (without **to**) is used to show possession.

I **have** a job.

GRAMMAR TASK: Find sentences with **have to/has to** in the photo story on pages 84–85.

Grammar in a Context

*Complete the sentences with **have, has, have to,** or **has to**.*

1. Margaret _____ a job. She works in an office.

2. Margaret _____ be Richard's partner.

3. Richard _____ an idea.

4. He tells Margaret that she _____ try to learn to dance.

5. It's eight o'clock. Richard and Margaret _____ a date.

Conversation

🎧 *Read and listen to the conversation.*

A: Let's go dancing tomorrow.
B: Sorry, I have to study tomorrow night.
A: Well, OK. Maybe some other time.
B: Why don't you ask Jerry? He always wants to go dancing.
A: Good idea.

🎧 *Listen again and practice.*

Vocabulary • Leisure Activities

🎧 *Look at the pictures. Say each phrase.*

go hiking   **go swimming**   **go Roller-blading**   **go skateboarding**   **go biking**   **go fishing**

Pair Practice

Practice the conversation and vocabulary with a partner. Use your own words.

A: Let's _____.

B: Sorry, I have to _____.

A: Well, OK. Maybe some other time.

B: Why don't you ask _____? _____ always wants to _____.

A: Good idea.

☑ **Now you know how to express obligations and regrets.**

 **Look at the first picture on page 95. With a partner, talk about the two men. What are they saying? Use your own words.**

SOCIAL LANGUAGE AND GRAMMAR 2

HOW TO **talk about ability/ask for help/express gratitude**

Can for Ability
Can expresses ability. Use *can* plus the base form of a verb. **A:** *Can* you *help* me? **B:** I'm sorry. I *can't help* you right now. Maybe later.

affirmative	negative
I *can write* that letter tonight.	I *can't go* skiing tomorrow.
Richard *can dance* the tango.	Sandy *cannot* come* to the party.

Can doesn't have *-s* in the third-person singular form.

TIP: Never use *to* immediately after *can*. (Don't say, "~~I can to help you~~".)

*cannot = can not

GRAMMAR TASK: Find sentences with *can* in the photo story on pages 84-85.

Grammar in a Context

*Complete the conversations with **can** or **can't** and the indicated verb.*

I _____ to the movies tonight, Paul.
1. go
I have to study for a psych test. Sorry.

I _____ you study, Liz.
2. help
I'm great at psychology.

When I meet a girl, I _____
3. think
of anything to say. Maybe that's why
I never have a date.

Call that computer dating service.
They _____ you a date.
4. find

Can: Questions

In questions, **can** comes before the subject of the sentence.

yes-no questions	possible answers
Can you go to the movies tonight?	No, I can't.
Can Robert really speak Russian?	Yes, he can.
Can Mary and George take me to the airport?	I don't know.

wh- questions	possible answers
When can I see you?	How about Wednesday evening?
Why can't you go hiking?	My ankle hurts.

GRAMMAR TASK: Answer two of the questions in your own words.

Conversation

🎧 *Read and listen to the conversation.*

A: What's the matter? You look worried.
B: This math homework is really hard. Can you help me?
A: Well, I can't right this minute. I have to go to the bank.
B: What about later? Please?
A: Sure.
B: Thanks a million.

🎧 *Listen again and practice.*

Vocabulary • Academic Subjects

🎧 *Look at the pictures. Say each word.*

calculus

English

chemistry

history

Pair Practice

Practice the conversation and vocabulary with a partner. Use your own words.

A: What's the matter? You look worried.

B: This _____ homework is really hard. Can you help me?

A: Well, I can't right this minute. I have to _____.

B: What about later? Please?

A: _____.

B: _____.

☑ **Now you know how to talk about ability, ask for help, and express gratitude.**

Grammar in a Context

*Complete the conversation with **can** or **can't** and the indicated words.*

This is Susan. May I help you?

Hi, Susan. This is Judy. Fluffy is sick. _____ me to the animal hospital
1. you / drive
sometime this morning?

My car's in the shop.

Why _____ her?
2. you / take

I'm working. _____ the office now!
3. I / leave

I don't know! Take a taxi. Take the bus. Walk.

Well, how _____ there?
4. I / get

Pronunciation
Can and Can't

🎧 *Read and listen to the following sentences.*

1. I can't dance.
2. Everybody can dance.
3. We can dance a tango.
4. Can you waltz?
5. She can't dance well.

🎧 *Now listen again and repeat.*

🎧 *Listen to these two sentences. What is different about the **a** sound in the underlined words?*

1. He <u>can</u> dance.
2. She <u>can't</u> dance.

🎧 *Listen to the sentences. Complete them with **can** or **can't**.*

1. I _____ play the piano.
2. I _____ speak Japanese but not Chinese.
3. She _____ read very well.
4. We _____ go now.

Improvise

Week at a Glance

	Morning	Afternoon	Evening
MONDAY		5:45 Dr. Smith	
TUESDAY			
WEDNESDAY			
THURSDAY			

Write your activities for next week in a date book like this one.

> **Examples:** doctor's appointments, dinner dates, sports (tennis games, etc.), classes.

Then, with a partner, make plans to do something together. If you can't meet, explain why:

> **A:** Sorry, I can't play tennis with you on Monday afternoon. I . . .
>
> **B:** Well, what about earlier (or that evening, etc.)?

Listening with a Purpose

Determine Context

Look at the chart with the question words.
🎧 *Listen to the conversation and think about those words. Take notes.*

Who?	Where?	What?

Circle the correct letter.

1. Who are the people?

   a. Sam and Doris   **b.** Paul and Liz   **c.** Richard and Margaret

2. Where are they?

   a. at the office   **b.** at a nightclub   **c.** at the movies

3. What are they doing?

   a. dancing   **b.** working   **c.** watching a movie

Ability Bingo

*(reinforces **can** + base form)*

Ask your classmates about their abilities. Find a person who can do each of these things. Write the classmate's name in the box.

As soon as you have four names in a row, say BINGO.

The first person to say BINGO wins.

speak French	play the guitar	ski	swim
read music	stand on your head	play the piano	type
speak Italian	touch your toes	water-ski	fix a car
do magic tricks	ice-skate	drive a truck	dance the samba

Sound Matches

*(reinforces **can / can't** pronunciation)*

*With a partner, think about the **Ability Bingo** game. Then make four cards with sentences with **can** and four cards with sentences with **can't**.*

*Take turns reading sentences to your partner. Your partner holds up a **CAN** or **CAN'T** card after each sentence.*

Watch your pronunciation!

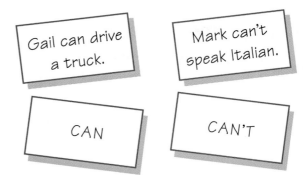

Gail can drive a truck.

Mark can't speak Italian.

CAN

CAN'T

Listening with a Purpose

Focus Attention

🎧 *Listen again to the conversation between Richard and Margaret. Listen specifically for names in their conversation.*

Now complete the following statements by circling the correct letter.

1. Richard's nickname is _____.
  a. Rich   **b.** Rick   **c.** Ripleys

2. Margaret's nickname is _____.
  a. Meg   **b.** Minnie   **c.** Maggie

3. The name of the band is _____.
  a. The Tantalizers   **b.** The Tambourines   **c.** The Tarantinos

4. The band is playing _____.
  a. tango music   **b.** rumba music   **c.** samba music

Bonus Question: What does Margaret mean when she says she has two left feet?

_____

_____

An Essay About Dancing

Before You Read: Look at the pictures. What are the people doing?

Read the essay. 🎧

rock

Dancing: Up Close or at a Distance?

Richard loves to dance, and he goes dancing often. Margaret is the opposite. She says she can't dance. Maybe that's true. She says people always laugh at her when she dances. But is it possible that there's another reason? Maybe she's afraid to dance. When you dance, you usually have to touch another person, your partner. Maybe Margaret is uncomfortable with touching.

Many people like dancing for its closeness. They like the waltz, the two-step, the fox-trot, and similar dances because they can be close to their partner. Other people like to dance in groups. They enjoy the group spirit in line dances, square dances, and folk dances. In these dances, touching your partner isn't very important. Working together as a group is.

Richard likes dances with specific steps, like the tango. He also likes "free" dances with no specific steps, like rock. Many people prefer free dances because they allow them to express their individuality.

But what about Margaret? What do you think? Do you think she really can't dance?

the tango   the waltz

a line dance

Comprehension: **Factual Recall**

Read the article again. Complete each sentence by circling the correct word or phrase.

1. One example of free dancing is (rock / the tango).

2. An example of close dancing is (group dancing / the waltz).

3. Line dances are (group dances / close dances).

4. An example of a dance with specific steps is (the tango / a free dance).

5. Some people prefer free dances because these dances (are close / allow personal expression).

In my opinion...   *I think...*   *because...*

Talk with a partner. Compare your opinions.

Do you like to go dancing?

In your opinion, why doesn't Margaret like dancing?

Why do you think Richard likes dancing?

I feel...   *I don't think...*   *What about you?*

Writing
A Newspaper Article

One Thing I Can Do Well Is ...

Pretend you are a student in a foreign country. Write an article about yourself for the student newspaper. Talk about your abilities. Use these questions and this newspaper article as a guide.

What can you do well?

How often do you do it?

Where do you do it?

Do you do it alone or with other people?

Do you have to practice?

The Ivy Leaves

Foreign Student News

Grace Mackey is new to the U this year. Read all about Grace.

Q. Please tell our readers something about yourself.

A. My name is Grace Mackey, and I'm from Australia. My family lives in the town of Cape Melville in the northeast part of the country.

Can you find Cape Melville on the map? If you can, then you can see that it is near the famous Great Barrier Reef. The Great Barrier Reef is very long. It extends almost two thousand kilometers along the coast.

In my school, all students have to learn how to swim. When I am at home, I swim two or three times a week. The beach is very near my house. It is a beautiful beach.

I often swim with my brothers. I have four brothers, and we all can swim very well. I never swim alone because there are a lot of sharks in Australian waters!

Warm up: Talk about these pictures with a partner. • Ask your partner questions. • Talk about the two men. • Where are they in the first picture? What are they doing? • Where are they in the second picture? What are they doing?

Then: Create conversations for the two men. OR Tell a story. Say as much as you can.

Unit 8

Do you want some pizza, Lulu?

Warm up: Look at the pictures. Say something to a partner about the boy. Listen. 🎧

1

2

3

4

Usually

Right Now

6

7

5

Comprehension: Factual Recall

🎧 *Listen to the story again. Complete each sentence by circling the correct letter.*

1. Joe doesn't go _____ every day.

    a. home   **b.** to school   **c.** to Luigi's

2. Joe doesn't go when there is going to be _____.

    a. problems   **b.** a test   **c.** a bad grade

3. Joe thinks his parents don't _____ him.

    a. worry about   **b.** like   **c.** listen to

4. One of Joe's special friends is _____.

    a. a dog   **b.** a teacher   **c.** a young woman

5. Lulu is _____.

    a. a person   **b.** a teacher   **c.** an animal

HOW TO get someone's attention/ask about price/agree to buy

Conversation

🎧 *Read and listen to the conversation.*

A: Excuse me.
B: Yes? How can I help you?
A: Do you have any umbrellas?
B: Sure. Right this way. . . .
A: I like this black one. How much is it?
B: Twelve dollars.
A: Twelve dollars? OK. I'll take it.

🎧 *Listen again and practice.*

Vocabulary • Clothing—Outerwear

🎧 *Look at the pictures. Say each word.*

 a raincoat

 a coat

 a jacket

 **an umbrella**

Vocabulary • Colors

🎧 *Look at the pictures. Say each word.*

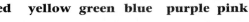

red **yellow** **green** **blue** **purple** **pink**

black **white** **brown** **gray** **beige** **orange**

Pair Practice

Practice the conversation and vocabulary with a partner. Use your own words.

A: Excuse me.

B: Yes? How can I help you?

A: Do you have any _____?

B: Sure. Right this way. . . .

A: I like this _____ one. How much is it?

B: _____.

A: _____? OK. I'll take it.

☑ **Now you know how to get someone's attention, ask for prices, and agree to buy.**

Some **and Any**

Use **some** in affirmative sentences.

> This store has **some** nice jackets.

Use **any** in negative sentences.

> No, we don't have **any** red umbrellas.

Use **some** or **any** in questions. The meanings are similar.

> Do you need **some** help? (*or* Do you need **any** help?)

TIP: Use **some** and **any** before non-count nouns or plural count nouns.

One **and Ones**

Which shirt do you like? I like that **one**.

What about the shoes? I like the black **ones**.

TIP: Use **one** to replace a singular count noun.
Use **ones** to replace a plural count noun.

GRAMMAR TASK: Make a list of five singular count nouns.

Grammar in a Context

Complete the conversation with the correct words.

I'm shopping for my grandson. It's his twenty-first birthday on Saturday, so I need _____
1. any / some
special presents. Do you have _____
2. a / any
nice ties?

The _____ over there
3. one / ones
are nice. How much are they?

Those? They're fifteen dollars.

They're really beautiful. I like this red _____.
4. one / ones

The green _____ is nice, too. I'll take them both.
5. one / ones

OK. Does your grandson need _____ shirts?
6. any / ones

There are _____ nice _____ on sale.
7. any / some   **8.** one / ones

Only twelve dollars this week.

No, he has lots of shirts. . . . Oh, I know. I see _____
9. any / some
raincoats over there. He really needs _____ raincoat.
10. a / any

OK. Anything else?

Hmm. Yes. He wants _____ baseball cap.
11. a / any

_____ baseball cap?
12. A / Some

Yes. Like the _____
13. one / any
that boy out there is wearing.

MEN'S SHOP

Look at the picture on page 107. With a partner, create conversations for the people in the picture. Use _some_ and _any_ and your own words.

Listening with a Purpose

Focus Attention 1

Alice is walking in the park after she goes shopping. She sees Joe Mason.

🎧 *Listen to the conversation between Joe and Alice. Listen specifically for the questions Alice asks Joe.*

🎧 *Now listen again and check the question in each pair that Alice asks Joe.*

1. ☐ Do you mind if I sit down here?
   ☐ Do you mind my sitting down here?

2. ☐ What's your name?
   ☐ What's her name?

3. ☐ Can I take a picture of you?
   ☐ Can I take a picture of you and Lulu?

4. ☐ Do you and Lulu live around here?
   ☐ Does Lulu live around here?

5. ☐ Don't you go to school?
   ☐ Do you go to school?

6. ☐ Really? Why that always?
   ☐ Really? Why not always?

Focus Attention 2

🎧 *Listen again to Joe and Alice's conversation. This time listen to Joe's answers to Alice's questions. Then complete the following statements.*

1. Alice sits down next to _____.

2. Lulu is the name of the _____.

3. Alice takes a picture of _____.

4. Joe _____ in the suburbs.

5. Joe _____ school.

HOW TO **state a need/express disbelief**

Conversation

🎧 *Read and listen to the conversation.*

A: How can I help you?

B: I need some boots.

A: Right over here. What size do you wear?

B: Size nine. I like these. How much are they?

A: Uh, let's see . . . A hundred and ten dollars.

B: You're kidding! A hundred and ten dollars for a pair of boots?

🎧 *Listen again and practice.*

Vocabulary • **Clothing That Comes in Pairs**

🎧 *Look at the pictures. Say each phrase.*

| (a pair of) **boots** | (a pair of) **gloves** | (a pair of) **mittens** | (a pair of) **socks** | (a pair of) **pants** | (a pair of) **shorts** |

This, These **and** That, Those

The plural of **this** is **these**:

> **This** dress is really pretty.
>
> **These shoes** are really nice, too.

The plural of **that** is **those**:

> **That** jacket is ugly! I hate **those** shirts, too.

T I P : Use **this** and **these** for things and people near you.

Use **that** and **those** for things and people distant from you.

Pair Practice

Practice the conversation and vocabulary with a partner. Use your own words.

A: How can I help you?

B: I need some _____.

A: _____. What size do you wear?

B: _____. I like these. How much are they?

A: Uh, let's see . . . They're _____.

B: You're kidding! _____ for a pair of _____?

☑ **Now you know how to state a need and express disbelief.**

Improvise

Here are some things you can buy at Butterworth's Department Store at the Valley Mall.

Form groups of four.

Group A: *You are the shoppers.*

Group B: *You work in the Men's Department at Butterworth's. Turn to page 145.*

Group C: *You work in the Women's Department at Butterworth's. Turn to page 145.*

Group D: *You work in the Shoe Department at Butterworth's. Turn to page 145.*

Group A: *You have $100 to spend at Butterworth's. Make a list of what you can buy for $100. Then go shopping.*

Reading
A Transcript of a Conversation

Before You Read: Sam and Doris are detectives. They look for people, animals, and things. They get information. Sometimes Joe Mason doesn't go to school. His parents are worried. Sam and Doris are helping Mr. and Mrs. Mason find out where Joe goes when he's not in school.

Look below at the title of this reading. Read to answer that question.
Read the conversation. 🎧

How Do You Know My Name?

Sam: Morning. Nice dog you've got there. Is she yours?

Joe: Uh, yeah, she's mine. . . . Why?

Sam: I'm a detective. My name's Sam Armstrong. And this is my partner, Doris Brand. We're looking for a missing dog. We have this picture, see? Your dog looks like the dog in the picture.

Doris: And what about you, son? It's nine o'clock. Aren't you going to school today?

Joe: Uh, no, . . . uh, I'm not.

Sam: How come?

Joe: Well, I don't go some days.

Doris: That's too bad. Teens need to go to school.

Joe: Most days I go.

Doris: Why not every day? It's hard to learn if you don't go.

Joe: I know. But sometimes I just need a day off.

Sam: Come on, Doris. We have to get back to the office.

Doris: So long, Joe.

Joe: So long . . . Uh, wait a minute. How do you know my name?

Doris: Your parents. They're worried about you. They want to know where you go when you don't go to school. We're helping them, Joe.

Joe: Really?

Doris: Really. They love you, Joe. You need to talk to them.

Joe: No, I can't talk to them. They don't understand.

Comprehension: Interpretation and Analysis

How can Sam and Doris know that the boy on the bench is Joe Mason?

Talk together as a group. Check your answer by looking at these pictures.

 **Look at the picture on page 107. Find Alice. Tell your partner what she's doing. Say as much as you can.**

Writing

A Conversation between Joe and His Parents

Read "How Do You Know My Name?" again. Write a conversation that Joe and his parents are going to have that night. Use the information in "How Do You Know My Name?" to help you write the conversation.

Example: **Mrs. Mason:** Joe, we're worried about you. Why aren't you going to school?

Joe: Well . . .

Heart to Heart

With a partner, talk about these questions.
Compare your opinions. Do you agree or disagree?

What are some problems between parents and
children? What can families do to communicate?

I think...   *In my opinion...*   *because...*

I feel...   *I don't think...*   *What about you?*

Pronunciation

/ɑ/ and /ʌ/

🎧 *Look at the pictures. Listen to the pronunciation
of these words.*

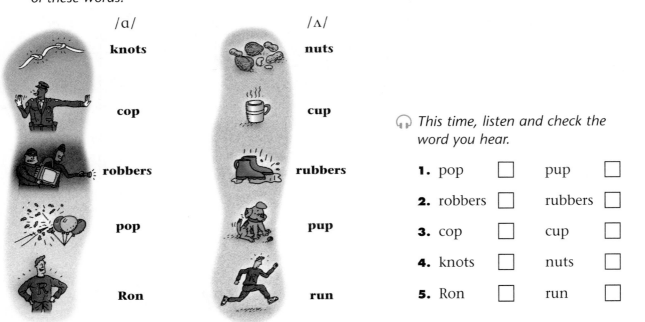

/ɑ/	/ʌ/
knots	nuts
cop	cup
robbers	rubbers
pop	pup
Ron	run

🎧 *This time, listen and check the
word you hear.*

1. pop ☐   pup ☐
2. robbers ☐   rubbers ☐
3. cop ☐   cup ☐
4. knots ☐   nuts ☐
5. Ron ☐   run ☐

🎧 *Now listen again and practice.*

Game

Minimal Pair Rummy

(reinforces pronunciation)

*Form two pairs of partners. Each person makes ten
cards, one for each word in the list above. One
person says a word without showing the card. His
or her partner holds up a card with the same
word. If the words match, the partners get a point.*

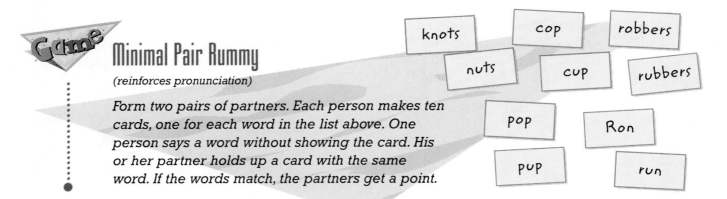

knots   cop   robbers
nuts   cup   rubbers
pop   Ron
pup   run

Warm up: Talk about this picture with a partner. • Ask your partner questions. • Talk about all the people. • What are they wearing? • What colors are their clothes? • What are the people doing? • What things do they have? • Talk about the animals in the picture.

Then: Create conversations for the people. OR Tell a story about the picture. Say as much as you can.

Unit 9 — Weren't you at Alice's?

Warm up: Look at the last picture in the photo story. Read the man's words. What do you think the people are talking about? Read or listen. 🎧

Hello?

Hello. May I speak to Julie Aronson?

This is Julie.

Hi. My name is Steven Costa. I'm in the Great Date program. And I guess you are too, and . . .

Oh. Yes. Hi.

So, I'm calling to, uh, ask if you want to . . . do something.

Oh. . . You know, your voice sounds really familiar.

That's funny. Yours does too.

Comprehension: Confirming Content

*Mark the following statements **true, false,** or **I don't know.***

		True	False	I don't know.
Example:	Steve plays soccer.	☑	☐	☐
1.	Julie is Charlie's girlfriend.	☐	☐	☐
2.	Julie is Steve's sister.	☐	☐	☐
3.	Julie was at Alice Mendoza's house about two weeks ago.	☐	☐	☐
4.	Steve is calling to ask Julie for a date.	☐	☐	☐
5.	Julie was Charlie's girlfriend years ago.	☐	☐	☐

HOW TO **talk about the past/give and accept an apology/ confirm identity**

The Past Tense of Be

Use **was** with **I, he, she,** or **it**.

> I **was** at the party last night.

Use **were** with **you, we,** and **they**.

> They **were** there, too.

Look at these negative sentences with **be**.

> She **was not (wasn't)** home last night.

> Steve and Julie **were not (weren't)** at the game.

The past form of **there is** is **there was**. The past form of **there are** is **there were**.

> **There was** a party last night. **There were** a lot of people at the party.

GRAMMAR TASK: Find and underline sentences with the past tense of **be** in the photo story on pages 108-109.

Grammar in a Context

Complete the sentences with **was, were, wasn't,** *or* **weren't.**

It _____ a terrible day. The weather _____
  1.   2.

terrible. Steve and Julie _____ at the movies.
                                    3.

The movie _____ boring. After the movie they
                  4.

_____ hungry. Unfortunately, Luigi's restaurant
   5.

_____ closed. The other restaurants _____
   6.   7.

open, either. It _____ a very good evening for
                          8.

Steve and Julie.

Look at the picture on page 119. Make true and false statements about the party on April 1. Use *there was, there were, there wasn't,* **and** *there weren't.* **Your partner corrects your false statements.**

The Past Tense of Be: Questions and Answers

yes-no questions	possible answers
Were you at home last night at eight?	Yes, I was.
Wasn't there a party on Saturday?	Yes, there was.
Was Julie at the party?	No. She was home in bed.

GRAMMAR TASK: Answer one question in your own words.

☑ **Now you know how to talk about the past.**

Conversation

Read and listen to the conversation.

A: Oops. Oh, excuse me.
B: That's OK. Don't worry.
A: No, really. I'm sorry about that. . . . By the way, I'm Millie Grant.
B: Hi, Millie. I'm Rod Lerner.
A: You know, you look really familiar. Weren't you at Laura's party the other night?
B: Yes, I was. Were you there, too?
A: Yeah. How do you know Laura?
B: She's my fiancée.

Listen again and practice.

Vocabulary • Past Time Expressions

Look at the picture. Say each word or phrase.

FEBRUARY

MONDAY	TUESDAY	WEDNESDAY	THURSDAY	FRIDAY	SATURDAY	SUNDAY
			1	2	3	4
5	6	7	8	9	10	11
12	13	14	15	16	17	18
19	20	21	22	23	24	25
26	27	28				

last week
last weekend
last Tuesday
the day before yesterday
yesterday
today

Vocabulary • Social and Business Relationships

🎧 *Look at the pictures. Say each word.*

boyfriend / girlfriend

fiancées

husband / wife

partners

boss / assistant

roommates

neighbors

Pair Practice

Practice the conversation and vocabulary with a partner. Use your own words.

A: Oops. Oh, excuse me.

B: That's OK. Don't worry.

A: No, really. I'm sorry about that. . . . By the way, I'm _____.

B: Hi, _____. I'm _____.

A: You know, you look really familiar. Weren't you at _____?

B: _____. Were you _____?

A: _____. How do you know _____?

B: _____.

☑ **Now you know how to give and accept an apology and confirm someone's identity.**

In Your Own Words Look at the picture of the party on April 15 on page 119. With a partner, create conversations for the people. Use your own words.

HOW TO **get information about the past**

The Past Tense of Be: Wh- Questions	
wh- questions	**possible answers**
Where *were* you last night?	We were at a concert until about ten.
Where *was* the party?	At Laura's.
Who *was* that man?	Just a guy from Great Date.
What *was* his name?	I think it was Jerry.
When *were* you home?	After the party.
Why *weren't* you here yesterday?	I was sick.

GRAMMAR TASK: Answer two of these questions in your own words.

Grammar in a Context

Complete the conversations with **was** *or* **were** *and the indicated words.*

Bob: Hey, Ted, _____ you were with at Jason's party?
   1. who / that girl

Ted: Oh, that was Emily Allen. She's Jason's cousin. Why?

Bob: She was gorgeous!

• • • • •

Amy: Am I doing OK in this class, Mary?

Mary: Well, Amy, now that you mention it, I'm not sure.

   What about the midterm test?

Amy: The midterm? Oh no! _____? Not yesterday!
   2. When / it

Mary: Yes, Amy. It was yesterday. _____ in class? Was something wrong?
   3. Why / you / not

Amy: I'm sorry, Mary. I was in the lab, . . . working for Dr. Dean.

• • • • •

Steve: Hello, Alice? This is Steve Costa. _____ for computer class?
   4. What / the homework

   I was sick yesterday.

Alice: We have to read Chapter Three and do the exercises at the end.

☑ **Now you know how to get information about the past.**

HOW TO talk about ownership and possession

Possessive Pronouns		
A: Whose shoes are these? Are they *yours*?		
B: Yes, they're *mine*.		

possessive pronouns	
mine	hers
yours	ours
his	theirs

TIP: Don't confuse possessive adjectives and possessive pronouns: Those are **my** shoes. Those are **mine**.

Grammar in a Context

Complete the conversations with the correct possessive pronouns or possessive adjectives.

Tom, whose dishes are these? Are they _____ or Nancy's?
1. your / yours

They're _____. _____ are on that table over there.
2. ours / our **3.** Hers / Her

No! Those dishes are _____.
4. mine / my
Nancy isn't selling any dishes.

OK. Look at all those bicycles. Sarah, what about that red one there? Is it _____ or Michael's?
5. your / yours

It's _____. _____ bike is really nice. I don't want to sell it.
6. his / hers **7.** My / Mine

Nancy, what about this bookcase? Is it Tom and Jane's? Or is it Linda's?

It's _____, I think.
8. theirs / their
Linda's not selling a bookcase.

☑ **Now you know how to talk about ownership and possession.**

Reading

A Conversation

Before You Read: Find and underline these phrases and sentences in the reading. Then, when you read, think about their meaning.

> would you like to   go Dutch   No way!   I can afford it.   It's not fair.

Read the conversation. 🎧

Out on a Date

Steve: Well, what would you like to see?

Julie: How about *Dance Fever*? I love musicals.

Steve: Me too. Great idea.

Julie: Yeah. But Steve, one thing—let's go Dutch. OK?

Steve: Go Dutch? No way! This is a date, and . . .

Julie: No, really. Guys always have to pay for everything. Movies are expensive. It's not fair.

Steve: But guys always pay. That's the way things are. I can afford it.

Julie: I'm sure you can afford it. That's not the point.

Steve: Tell you what. Let me pay this time. You can pay next time. OK?

Julie: Promise?

Steve: Promise.

Comprehension: Understanding Meaning from Context

Circle the letter that correctly explains the meaning of each sentence or question.

1. What would you like to see?

  a. What do you want to see?   **b.** What do we see?

2. Let's go Dutch. OK?

  a. You pay. OK?   **b.** Let's each pay for ourselves.

3. No way!

  a. I don't want to.   **b.** I don't know how.

4. It's not fair.

  a. It's cheap.   **b.** It's not right.

5. I can afford it.

  a. I don't have enough money.   **b.** I have enough money.

Heart to Heart

Talk about these questions with a partner. Compare your opinions.

If you go on a date, who pays?

If you go out with a group of people, who pays?

What do you think about going Dutch? Is it a good idea?

What is the custom today? Was it different years ago?

I feel...   *I don't think...*   *What about you?*

Writing

A Paragraph about Dating

Think about your discussion in Heart to Heart. Choose one of the questions and write your ideas in a paragraph. In your first sentence, tell the reader what the topic of the paragraph is. That sentence is a topic sentence. Use the other sentences in the paragraph to explain your ideas.

Indent the first sentence.

Example:

> Today, when I go out on a date, I like to go Dutch. Movies and restaurants are expensive, and I can afford to pay. It's not fair for one person to pay all the time.

Listening with a Purpose

Focus Attention

You are going to hear a telephone conversation about a date. Read these questions.

1. Who are the two speakers? _____

2. Where were they last night? _____

3. Was the man mad? _____

4. Was he quiet? _____

5. Who is going to pay for dinner tonight? _____

🎧 *Now listen to find the answers.*

Improvise

Read the Conversation on page 111 again. Listen to the phone conversation in Listening with a Purpose on page 116 again. Then, with a partner, improvise a conversation that includes an apology.

Pronunciation
The /r/ and /h/ Sounds

🎧 *Look at these words and listen to their pronunciation.*

hat   **rat**   **hope**   **rope**

🎧 *Listen again and repeat.*

> **TIP:** To say the /r/, put the sides of your tongue against your upper back teeth. The tip of your tongue doesn't touch anything.

Dictation 1

🎧 *Listen. Write the words that you hear.*

1. _____   **2.** _____

Pronunciation
The /r/ and /l/ Sounds

🎧 *Look at these words and listen to their pronunciation.*

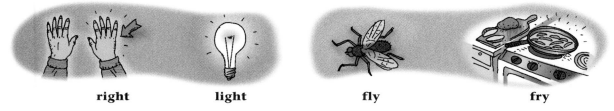

right   **light**   **fly**   **fry**

> **TIP:** To say the /l/, put the tip of your tongue on the top of your mouth, behind your teeth. Say the sound quickly and then stop.

🎧 *Listen again and repeat.*

Dictation 2

🎧 *Listen. Write the words that you hear.*

1. _____   2. _____

  Pronunciation

The /r/, /d/, and /t/ Sounds

🎧 *Look at these words and listen to their pronunciation.*

Terri   **Teddy**   **berry**   **Betty**

🎧 *Listen again and repeat.*

Dictation 3

🎧 *Listen. Write the words that you hear.*

1. _____   2. _____

Practice

🎧 *Listen to the following words and sentences. Repeat them after the speaker. Then practice them with a partner.*

1. Ron runs every day.
2. The rats are running.
3. Those hats are ridiculous.

4. The right light is out.
5. Teddy is writing.
6. Teddy hopes Terri is right.

 Minimal Pair Rummy

(reinforces / r / contrasts)

Form two pairs of partners. Each person makes twelve cards, one for each of these words. One partner says a word without showing the card. His or her partner holds up a card with the same word. If the words match, the partners get a point.

fly	fry	Terry	Teddy
hat	rat	hope	rope
Berry	Betty	right	light

Warm up: Talk about these pictures with a partner.
• What is happening? • What are some of the people doing?
• What time is it? • What is the date? • What things are in the pictures?

Then: Create conversations for the people. OR Tell a story about the pictures. Say as much as you can.

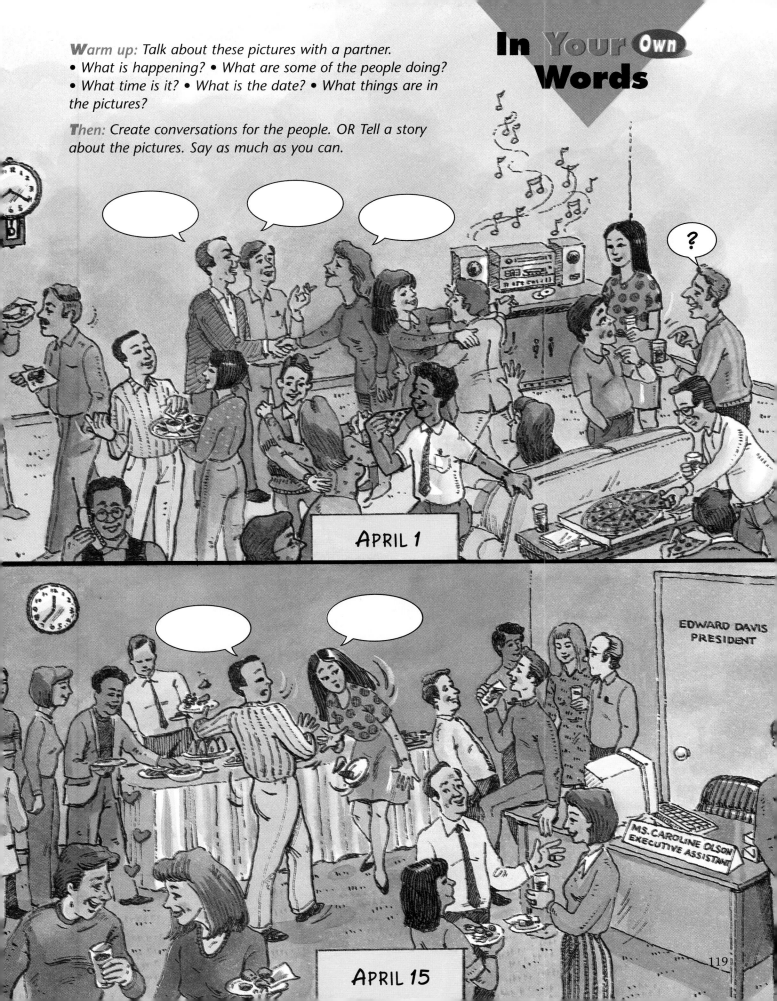

Receptive Model

Warm up: Look at the pictures. Where are the two women?
Read or listen. 🎧

This is Diana. May I help you?

Hey, Babe! Guess who?

Daphne!

You bet! Your long-lost sister. Guess what? I'm back.

Daphne, this is great! Where are you?

At the airport. My plane landed half an hour ago, and I just got my luggage.

Gee, Daph, why didn't you let me know you were coming? I'm at the office. I can't pick you up right now.

Well, I thought you needed a surprise. But don't worry. I can take a taxi.

OK. Great. . . . Uh-oh, got to go. I have to take another call. It's probably Sandy again.

Who?

Sandy. My crazy next-door neighbor. She's having another crisis.

Oh. Yeah. Sandy. You told me about her. Well, see you later.

Comprehension: Factual Recall

Circle the correct letter.

1. Who is Sandy?

   a. Diana's neighbor   **b.** Diana's boss

2. Where was Daphne for four years?

   a. in the army   **b.** at the office

3. Who are Daphne and Diana?

   a. next-door neighbors   **b.** sisters

HOW TO **talk about past actions and facts**

The Simple Past Tense

Use the simple past tense to talk about past actions and facts.

> Daphne's plane landed half an hour ago.
>
> Diana talked to her on the phone.

To form the simple past tense of a regular verb, add **-ed** to the base form. If the base form ends in **-e**, add **-d**. If the base form ends in a consonant plus **y**, change the **y** to **i** and add **-ed.**

base form	simple past
play	played
practice	practiced
study	studied

Form questions in the simple past tense with the auxiliary **did** + subject + base form.

> auxiliary   subject   base form
>
> **Did   Diana's phone   ring**   last night?

Form negative statements in the simple past with **did** + **not (didn't)** + base form.

> auxiliary   base form
>
> We   **didn't   take**   a vacation last year.

The Simple Past Tense: Some Irregular Forms

base form	simple past	base form	simple past
come	came	hear	heard
do	did	know	knew
feel	felt	make	made
find	found	meet	met
forget	forgot	say	said
get	got	see	saw
go	went	take	took
grow	grew	tell	told
have	had	think	thought

TIP: To show ability (**can**) in the past, use **could** + the base form.

> Daphne said she **could** take a taxi.

GRAMMAR TASK: Find and underline regular and irregular past forms in the photo story on pages 120–121.

Grammar in a Context

*Complete the conversation with simple past tense forms or with **did** or **didn't**.*

Daphne: What about all our old friends? What are they up to?

Diana: Well, let's see. Stan _____ to Miami about two years ago. Patty _____
                  1. move   **2. go**

to Kansas City to be with her mother. Sam and Jane are still living here.

Sam _____ his own detective agency about three years ago. Jane stays
       3. open

home with the kids. Oh, and Maggie has a boyfriend—a guy named Richard.

They _____ at work, and they _____ dating a few weeks ago.
       4. meet   **5. start**

Daphne: What about you? Any new men in your life?

Diana: Not right now. . . . But tell me this: Why did you come back?

I thought you _____ this place.
             6. like

Daphne: No, I always _____ it here. I just _____ to get away for a while.
               7. like   **8. want**

Diana: Are you back to stay?

Daphne: I think so. . . . Hey, I've got a great idea. Remember in high school when we

_____ tricks on the other kids, and they _____ we were twins?
   9. play   **10. know**

Well, let's play one on Sandy!

These girls are twins. They are playing a trick on their classmates.

☑ **Now you know how to talk about past actions and facts.**

Pronunciation

Past Tense Endings: worked / played / repeated

🎧 *Listen to the pronunciation of these past tense verbs. Listen for the last sound: /t/*

　　　liked　　　　　practiced　　　　kissed

🎧 *Listen again and repeat.*

🎧 *Listen to the pronunciation of these past tense verbs. Listen for the last sound: /d/*

　　　happened　　　　played　　　　　moved

🎧 *Listen again and repeat.*

🎧 *Listen to the pronunciation of these past tense verbs. Listen for the last sound: /ɪd/*

　　　wanted　　　　　needed　　　　　waited

TIP: If the last letter in a regular past tense verb is *t* or *d*, pronounce the ending as *id.*

🎧 *Listen again and repeat.*

🎧 *Listen to these verbs and sentences. Repeat them after the speaker. Then, working with a partner, practice pronouncing the verbs and sentences.*

1. practiced　　　　　I practiced the piano yesterday.

2. kissed　　　　　　Julie kissed her mother.

3. played　　　　　　Rick and Maggie played volleyball yesterday.

4. moved　　　　　　Patty moved away two years ago.

5. waited　　　　　　Alice waited for the bus for an hour.

6. needed　　　　　　Steve needed help in computer class.

SOCIAL LANGUAGE AND GRAMMAR 2

How to **talk about recent activities/empathize**

Conversation

🎧 *Read and listen to the conversation.*

A: Hello?

B: Hi, Mandy. Guess who?

A: Jim? When did you get back?

B: Yesterday morning.

A: So how was Mexico?

B: Terrific. We played tennis, and we went swimming every day. And the food was great, too.

A: Sounds like you had a great time.

🎧 *Listen again and practice.*

Vocabulary • More Past Time Expressions

🎧 *Look at the pictures. Say each phrase.*

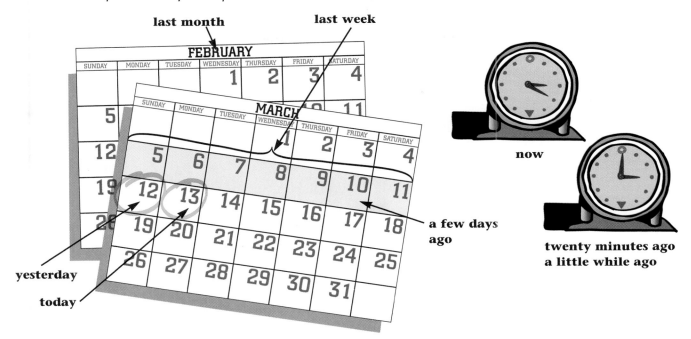

last month

last week

now

a few days ago

twenty minutes ago
a little while ago

yesterday

today

Pair Practice

Practice the conversation and vocabulary with a partner.
Use your own words.

A: Hello?

B: Hi, _____. Guess who?

A: _____? When did you get back?

B: _____.

A: So how was _____?

B: _____. We _____.

A: Sounds like you had a _____ time.

☑ **Now you know how to talk about recent activities and empathize with someone's feelings.**

 **Look at the pictures on page 131. With two partners, create a conversation for the three people looking at the photos. Use your own words.**

Improvise

Tell a partner about a trip you took. Say as much as you can. Your partner asks you questions.

Reading

An Article about Twins

Before You Read: *Find and circle these words and phrases in the reading. When you read, think about their meaning.*

look alike	environment	heredity	grew up

Read the article. 🎧

Modern Woman	May 26

Behind Your Horoscope
This month's sign is Gemini—The Twins

How Much Do You Know about Twins?

About eleven of every one thousand births are twins. That means that about one of every fifty people has a twin.

There are two types of twins: fraternal and identical. Fraternal twins can be of the same sex or can be brother and sister. Sometimes they look alike, with the same hair and eye color, for example. Sometimes they do not look alike. Identical twins look exactly alike. They are always of the same sex.

What makes people the way they are? Is it the environment? For example, can an unhappy home create an unhappy person? Or is it heredity? Or is it both?

Think about two identical twins named Jim Lewis and Jim Springer. They were born in 1940. They grew up in different families and found each other when they were thirty-nine. As boys, both had a dog named Toy. Both men were six feet tall. Both weighed

126   UNIT 10

180 pounds. Both were married two times—the first time to a woman named Linda, and the second time to a woman named Betty. Jim Lewis named his first son James Alan, and Jim Springer named his first son James Allen. Both had the same job. They both liked to eat and drink the same things.

How can we explain this true story?

Comprehension: Understanding Meaning from Context

Circle the choice with the same meaning as the numbered sentence or question.

1. Sometimes fraternal twins look alike.

    a. Sometimes fraternal twins look the same.
    b. Sometimes fraternal twins look nice.

2. What makes people the way they are? Is it the environment?

    a. Is it people's experiences?
    b. Is it people's twins?

3. Is it heredity?

    a. Is it people's experiences?
    b. Is it people's parents, grandparents, great-grandparents, etc.?

4. They grew up in different families.

    a. They spent their early years in different families.
    b. They married into different families.

Comprehension: Factual Recall

*Mark the following statements **true** or **false**.*

	True	False
1. Fraternal twins always look alike.	☐	☐
2. Identical twins are always of the same sex.	☐	☐
3. Jim Lewis and Jim Springer grew up in different families.	☐	☐
4. Both Jim Lewis and Jim Springer married the same woman.	☐	☐
5. Both Jim Lewis and Jim Springer liked to eat and drink the same things.	☐	☐

Heart to Heart

I think... *In my opinion...* *because...*

With a partner, discuss these questions.
Compare your opinions.

What makes us the way we are? The environment? Heredity? Both? Can an unhappy home make an unhappy person?

I feel... *I don't think...* *What about you?*

Listening with a Purpose

Determine Context

The story has three parts. Look at the pictures for each of the three parts.

🎧 *Listen to the story. As you listen, write the name of each person below her picture.*

_____   _____   _____

🎧 *Now listen again and circle the answer to each of the following questions.*

1. Who are the three people talking?
   a. Fifi, Diana, and Daphne   **b.** Sandy, Diana, and Daphne

2. Where are they?
   a. at Diana's house   **b.** at Sandy's house

3. Who are Diana and Daphne?
   a. friends   **b.** sisters

4. What are they doing?
   a. helping Sandy   **b.** playing a trick on Sandy

5. What's the surprise?
   a. Diana and Daphne are twins.   **b.** Diana and Daphne are selling things to Sandy.

HOW TO get information about the past

The Simple Past Tense: Wh- Questions	
wh- questions	**possible answers**
What did you do last night?	We went to a movie.
Why didn't you let me know?	I didn't know until today.
When did she finish school?	Two years ago. She went to school after the army.
What happened to Diana?	I don't know. Did something happen?
How many languages could you speak when you were a child?	Two. English and Spanish. I couldn't speak Portuguese until I was twelve.

GRAMMAR TASK: Answer the first and last questions in your own words.

Grammar in a Context

Complete the questions and negatives in the simple past tense, using the indicated words.

Sandy: OK. Now I want an answer. Diana,

_____ me you had a twin?
1. why / you / not / tell

Diana: Well, it just _____ to me.
2. not / occur

Sandy: I _____ what was happening.
3. not / understand
And I was pretty mad.

Diana: Are you still mad?

Sandy: Oh, I guess not. But _____ it?
4. why / you / do

Diana: Oh, just for fun. You need a little

humor in your life. You were so funny!

Rick: I've got a question. _____ you guys _____ tricks on people
5. Do   **6.** play

when you were in school?

Daphne: Yep, we did. Some of the kids _____ we were twins. And they
7. not / know

_____ tell us apart.
8. can / not

Maggie: I've got a question, too. Daphne, why do you call Diana "Babe"?

Daphne: Because she's the baby. She was born twenty minutes after me.

Did You Tell the Truth?

(reinforces getting information about the past)

Choose three contestants: Contestant A, Contestant B, and Contestant C. The class has to guess which contestant was the real John F. Kennedy, a famous U.S. president.

Here is a list of questions to ask each contestant. Write each answer on this chart.

● *Contestants A, B, and C, turn to page 145 for your answers.*

Questions	A	B	C
1. What was your name?			
2. When were you born?			
3. How many brothers and sisters did you have?			
4. Where did you grow up?			
5. Could you play football well when you were a child?			
6. Did you fight in World War II?			
7. Were you in politics before you were president?			
8. How many times were you married?			
9. How many children did you have?			
10. When were you president of the United States?			
11. Were you young or old when you died?			
12. Where did you die?			
13. What was your wife's name?			

☑ **Now you know how to get information about the past.**

Writing

A Description of a Famous Person

Choose a famous person. Use the questions in "Did You Tell the Truth?" for ideas. Write about your famous person.

Your classmates guess who the person is.

Warm up: Talk about the pictures with a partner. • Where is the man in each picture? • Where did he go? • What is he wearing? • Talk about the time of each picture. • What else do you see in the pictures? How many things can you name?

Then: Create conversations for the people. OR Tell a story about the pictures. Say as much as you can.

131

Review, SelfTest, and Extra Practice

Part 1

Review

I Have to Work Late

Sam Armstrong is a detective. Jane is his wife. Sometimes Sam has to work late.

🎧 *Listen to the telephone conversation between Sam and Jane.*

SelfTest

Grammar: Verb Review

Here is a transcript of Sam and Jane's conversation. Choose the correct word or phrase to complete each blank.

Jane: Hello?

Sam: Hi, honey. Listen, I . . .

Jane: Sam, where _____ you? It's 6:30. I just _____ dinner on the table.
           1. are / were   **2.** putting / put

      The kids _____ right now.
          3. eat / are eating

Sam: I know Jane. I'm sorry, but I _____ work late. Something _____ up.
                                    4. have / have to   **5.** comes / came

Jane: But Sam, we _____ concert tickets for tonight. _____ you
                                  6. have / have to   **7.** Don't / Doesn't

        remember? Your mother _____ be here any minute now.
                                         8. is / is going to

Sam: Oh, no! _____ the concert tonight?
                       9. Is / Are

Jane: Yes, dear. _____ tonight.
                     10. It's / Is

Sam: I _____ on a case. I just _____ leave now. Sorry.
                11. 'm working / work   **12.** can / can't

Jane: Sam, sometimes I think you're married to your job.

Sam: Why don't you ask Maggie to go with you? She _____ concerts.
                                                            13. like / likes

Jane: Well . . . I _____ Maggie yesterday, but she _____ home. I think
                     14. called / call   **15.** was / wasn't

        she _____ out of town.
                    16. goes / went

Sam: Call her again. Maybe _____ back.
                                17. she was / she's

Jane: Well, OK.

Sam: I'm sorry, Jane. I _____ go. Talk to you later. I _____ you. Bye.
                          18. have to / have   **19.** love / loved

Jane: Bye.

Bonus **Question:** Jane says to Sam, "Sometimes I think you're married to your job."
                                       What does Jane mean?

_____

Improvise

Work with a partner. One person telephones and reminds the second person about an event they are going to attend. The second person apologizes and says he or she has to do something else and can't go. Then that person suggests asking someone else.

Extra Practice

The Green-Eyed Monster

by Ken Whitman

🎧 *Read or listen to the magazine article.*

Imagine the scene. There's a new baby in the house. Jerry is four years old. His little sister was born a week ago, and she just came home from the hospital yesterday. Everyone loves her. Everyone is watching her. No one is watching Jerry or talking to him. Jerry is angry. He hates his little sister. What's Jerry's problem? It's the green-eyed monster. Jerry is jealous.

Now picture this scene. Jennifer is eighteen years old. Tom is her boyfriend, and Jennifer and Tom like each other a lot. But one day Jennifer sees Tom talking to another girl. They're smiling and having a good time. Jennifer can't believe her eyes. She begins to get mad. That night, she calls Tom and says, "Who was that girl you were with today?"

"What girl?" Tom asks.

"I saw you with a girl on the street."

"Oh, that was Laura. She's my next-door neighbor."

Jennifer doesn't believe Tom. She's very angry. She says, "I never want to see you again," and hangs up the phone. It's the green-eyed monster again. Jennifer is jealous.

Now picture a third scene. Mark is in his forties. He's good friends with Joe, and they do a lot of things together. They both work in an office. One day, Mark hears Joe inviting Bill, another employee, to play cards with him that night. Mark is hurt. "Why didn't Joe invite me to play cards?" Mark thinks. "Joe and I are best friends." The green-eyed monster is here again. Mark is jealous.

Is jealousy normal? Probably. Is it good? Not usually. It's easy to become jealous, but it's hard to solve the problems that jealousy causes. Jealousy can hurt relationships. Maybe the best thing to do when we're feeling jealous is just to tell the green-eyed monster to leave.

Comprehension: Drawing Conclusions

Read or listen to "The Green-Eyed Monster" again. Complete each sentence by circling the correct letter.

1. When we are jealous of other people, we _____.

   a. don't like them   **b.** like them   **c.** want what they have

2. The green-eyed monster is _____.

   a. a real monster   **b.** a good feeling we have   **c.** a bad feeling we have

3. The author thinks jealousy is _____.

   a. OK   **b.** usually a good thing   **c.** usually a bad thing

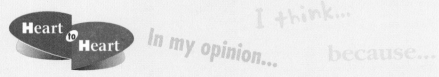

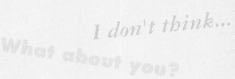

With a partner, discuss these questions.

Is jealousy a problem for you?

How can a person make jealousy go away?

I think...

In my opinion...

because...

I feel...

I don't think...

What about you?

How Was Your Date?

Bob Mercer and Amy Lane are students.

🎧 *Read and listen to their conversation in the library.*

Comprehension: Confirming Content

🎧 *Read or listen to "How Was Your Date?" again. Then mark the following statements* **true, false,** *or* **I don't know.**

		True	False	I don't know.
1.	Amy is Bob's girlfriend.	☐	☐	☐
2.	Sally has two boyfriends.	☐	☐	☐
3.	Sally is angry at Bob.	☐	☐	☐
4.	Bob is angry at Sally.	☐	☐	☐
5.	Bob knows the boy Sally was with.	☐	☐	☐
6.	Bob believes he was wrong.	☐	☐	☐

Writing

Pretend you are Bob. Write a note to Sally. Apologize.
Explain. Ask to get together.

Extra Practice

Part 4

Review

I Need to Make an Appointment.

Steve Costa is an athlete. He is calling the doctor's office to make an appointment.

🎧 *Listen to Steve's conversation with the doctor's secretary.*

Comprehension: Factual Recall

🎧 *Read these statements. Then listen again to the telephone conversation. Complete each sentence by circling the correct letter.*

1. Steve's _____ hurts.
   a. knee   **b.** back   **c.** ankle

2. Steve plays _____.
   a. baseball   **b.** soccer   **c.** football

3. Steve's game is _____.
   a. next Friday   **b.** next Saturday **c.** next Sunday

4. Tomorrow afternoon Steve is going to be _____ until five.
   a. at work   **b.** at home   **c.** in class

5. Steve's appointment is Friday morning at _____.
   a. 10:15   **b.** 10:30   **c.** 10:50

Extra Practice

Pair Practice

Make a doctor's appointment with a partner. Use this conversation as a guide.

A: _____ office. How may I help you?

B: This is _____. I need _____.

A: OK. What's the problem?

B: _____.

A: All right. How about _____? Is that good for you?

B: Sorry, I'm going to _____.

A: OK. How about _____?

B: Yes, that's fine.

Part 5

Review

What Does Mom Want for Her Birthday?

Joe Mason is a teenager. He and his father are shopping for Mrs. Mason's birthday present.

🎧 *Look at the pictures. Predict the story. Then listen to the conversation between Joe and his father.*

SelfTest

Grammar

🎧 *Now listen to the conversation again. Choose the correct word to complete each sentence.*

Mr. Mason: Thanks for coming, Joe. Two heads are better than one.

Joe: Sure, Dad. What does Mom want for her birthday, anyway?

Mr. Mason: I don't know, Joe. Maybe a dress? Or a bathing suit?

Joe: Yeah, both of _____ sound good.
           1. that / those

Salesperson: May I help you?

Mr. Mason: Yes, we're looking for a birthday present for my wife. We're not sure if we

want to buy _____ dress or a bathing suit.
                2. a / any

Salesperson: We don't have _____ bathing suits in this department, but we
                                  3. some / any

have _____ very nice dresses over there. Do you know your
              4. some / any

wife's size?

Mr. Mason: Her size? Gosh, I don't know. Do you know, Joe?

Joe: No, I don't know, Dad.

Salesperson: We need her size for a dress. . . . Hmm. How about a pair of gloves?

We have some nice _____ over here.
                          5. one / ones

Mr. Mason: What do you think, Joe?

Joe: Mom doesn't wear gloves, does she?

Salesperson: How about a scarf? Here's a beautiful _____. It's on sale for $25.00.
                                       6. one / ones

Mr. Mason: Yes, a scarf's a great idea. What do you think, Joe? I like that green

and yellow _____.
              7. one / ones

Joe: Yeah, but I really like this pink and purple _____.
                                          8. one /ones

Mr. Mason: Yes, I do too. How much is that scarf?

Salesperson: Let's see. . . . That _____ is $8.95.
                        9. one / ones

Mr. Mason: OK. We'll take it. . . . Your mom is going to love this scarf, Joe.

Joe: Yeah, she sure is!

Bonus Question: Joe's father says, "Two heads are better than one."
What does he mean?

Improvise

One partner is a customer, and the other is a salesperson. Improvise a conversation in a department store about buying a present for someone. Ask about different items and prices.

SOCIAL LANGUAGE SelfTest

Circle the appropriate statement or question to complete each of the following conversations.

1. A: Sorry, I can't go dancing on Friday.

   B: _____

     a. Why don't you ask Bill?   **c.** Let's go hiking.

     b. OK. Maybe some other time.   **d.** When?

2. A: What's the matter?

   B: _____

     a. I'm Meg Ford. Glad to meet you.   **c.** Well, not really.

     b. How may I help you?   **d.** My knee hurts.

3. A: _____

   B: Sure. Right over there.

     a. Do you need to see Dr. Taylor?   **c.** Is that good for you?

     b. Do you have any men's boots?   **d.** Excuse me.

4. A: May I help you?

   B: _____

     a. My name is Amy Lane.   **c.** Yes, I can be there this afternoon.

     b. Not usually.   **d.** Yes, I need to make an appointment with Doctor Starr.

5. A: Do you have a minute?

B: _____

    a. Sorry, I can't.   **c.** Why don't you ask Richard?

    b. Sure. What's up?   **d.** It's ten after six.

6. A: So how was your trip to Hawaii?

B: _____

    a. We went to Hawaii.   **c.** Last year.

    b. Great.   **d.** Two weeks.

7. A: Pick you up at seven. Where do you live?

B: _____

    a. In Vancouver.   **c.** 312 Laramie Lane.

    b. In an apartment.   **d.** I don't live there anymore.

8. A: _____

B: OK. I'll take it.

    a. It's thirty dollars.   **c.** Do you have any umbrellas?

    b. How much is it?   **d.** These shoes are really comfortable.

9. A: Do you see any dresses you like?

B: _____

    a. Well, what about later?   **c.** I don't like that.

    b. Yes, I really like that green one.   **d.** Do you have any dresses?

10. A: Can you see Doctor Starr at 4:30?

B: _____

    a. No, I need to see him.   **c.** My back hurts.

    b. Yes, 6:30.   **d.** No, I'm going to be in a meeting until five.

11. A: How do you know Alison?

    B: _____

        a. Her name is Alison.   **c.** She's an excellent student.

        b. Alison doesn't live here anymore.   **d.** She's my fiancée.

12. A: Why didn't you call and tell me you were in town?

    B: _____

        a. How long are you going to be here?   **c.** I tried, but no one answered the phone.

        b. I didn't.   **d.** I'm going to be in town for three days.

13. A: _____

    B: Hi. I'm Anne Bramson.

        a. Were you at the party?   **c.** By the way, I'm Rachel Crowe.

        b. You know, he looks really familiar.   **d.** That was Jason's cousin.

14. A: Sorry about last night.

    B: _____

        a. Do you mean last night?   **c.** You weren't there last night.

        b. That's OK.   **d.** Are you angry?

15. A: Hi, Rod. Guess who?

    B: _____

        a. Terrific. We played tennis.   **c.** Well, how about later?

        b. In New York.   **d.** Millie.

Activity Links for 1A and 1B

Unit 2

Crazy Backwards Questions

Partner B: Listen to Partner A's answers. When Partner A reads you an answer, read him or her a question from this list.

How are these books?
Are you a student?
What time is it?
Where's the concert?
Who's the teacher?

Now here is a list of five answers. Read each one to Partner A. Partner A gives you a question for each answer.

That's the teacher.
No, there isn't.
I'm fine.
Daughters of Dracula.
No, he's single.

Unit 4

Lost in Cascadia

Partner B: Partner A is lost and calls you for directions. Look at your map. Give Partner A directions.

Example:

A: Hello, _____? This is _____. I'm a little lost. I'm going to the Cascadia Art Museum. Right now I'm at a gas station at the corner of Baltic Avenue and Main Street.

B: No problem. Go down _____ to . . .

Switch roles with Partner A.
Get directions to another place.

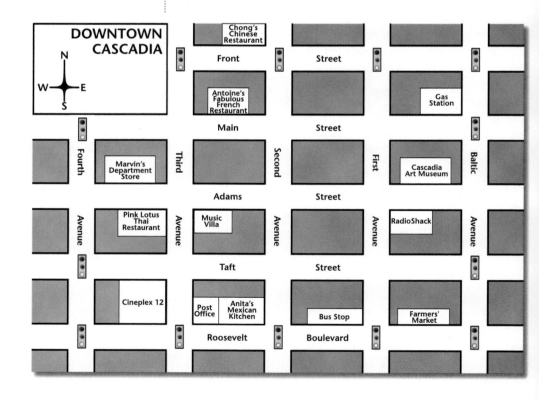

Unit 8

Improvise

Group B: Here are some items in the Men's Department. Tell Group A the prices of the things they want to buy. Have conversations.

bathing suit	$15
belt	$12
blue jeans	$24
boxer shorts	$8
briefs	$5
dress shirt	$18
pajamas	$15
sport shirt	$12
suit	$75
sweater	$20
tie	$16
T-shirt	$10
undershirt	$5

Group C: Here are some items in the Women's Department. Tell Group A the prices of things they want to buy. Have conversations.

belt	$12
bikini	$25
blouse	$18
bra	$12
dress	$50
nightgown	$15
one-piece bathing suit	$25
panty hose	$8
panties	$8
skirt	$30
slacks	$50

Group D: Here are some items in the Shoe Department. Tell Group A the prices of things they want to buy. Have conversations.

boots	$100
loafers	$36
men's dress shoes	$80
running shoes	$45
sandals	$24
slippers	$30
women's dress shoes	$50

Unit 10

To Tell the Truth

Contestant A: Here is the information you need to answer the questions. (You are not telling the truth.)

1. My name was John F. Kennedy.
2. I was born in 1898.
3. I had nine brothers and sisters.
4. I grew up in New York.
5. No, I could not.
6. No, I didn't.
7. Yes, I was vice president.
8. I was married two times.
9. We had one child.
10. I was president from 1956 to 1960.
11. I was old when I died.
12. I died in Miami.
13. Her name was Jessie.

Contestant B: Here is the information you need to answer the questions. (You are telling the truth.)

1. My name was John F. Kennedy.
2. I was born in 1917.
3. I had eight brothers and sisters.
4. I grew up in Massachusetts.
5. Yes, I could.
6. Yes, I did.
7. Yes, I was a senator.
8. I was married once.
9. We had two children.
10. I was president from 1961 to 1963.
11. I was young when I died.
12. I died in Dallas, Texas.
13. Her name was Jackie.

Contestant C: Here is the information you need to answer the questions. (You are not telling the truth.)

1. My name was John F. Kennedy.
2. I was born in 1910.
3. I had six brothers and sisters.
4. I grew up in Florida.
5. No, I could not.
6. No, I didn't.
7. Yes, I was a governor.
8. I was married three times.
9. We had four children.
10. I was president from 1965 to 1968.
11. I was old when I died.
12. I died in Boston.
13. Her name was Jenny.

Appendices for 1A and 1B

Key Vocabulary

This unit-by-unit vocabulary list shows key words and expressions presented for students' active use. The definite or indefinite article is included to help students with usage.

Unit 1

Nouns

an adult
an animal
an artist
a character
a class
a doctor
an engineer
a friend
a homemaker
a human
a lawyer
a man
a manager
a name
a neighbor
a nurse
a party
a secretary
a student
a superhero
a teacher
a teenager
a woman

Verb: Be

am
is
are

Adjectives

athletic
boring
easy
fictional
great
hard
historical
interesting
married
old
real
short
single
studious
tall
young

Adverb

not

Articles

a
an
the

Subject Pronouns

I
you
he
she
it
we
you
they

Contractions

he's
I'm
we're
you're
they're
she's
it isn't
she isn't
we aren't

Wh- words

what's
who's

Expressions

Nice to meet you.
Nice to meet you, too.

Unit 2

Nouns

the afternoon
a cat
a concert
the evening
maps
the morning
a movie
a play
the time

Days of the Week

Monday
Tuesday
Wednesday
Thursday
Friday
Saturday
Sunday

Count and Non-count Nouns

a car
a dog
an elephant
an orange

bread
milk
snow
water

Verbs

go
want

Adjectives

excited
fine
good
OK
terrific

Adverbs

maybe
today
tomorrow
tonight

Wh- words

what
when
why

Prepositions

at
in
on

Expressions

How are you?
See you later.
See you there.
That's great.

Other

there is
there are
there's

Unit 3

Nouns

an address
a cassette player
a CD player
a computer
a fax machine
a laptop
a message
a play
a phone number
pizza
a restaurant
a remote
a TV
a walk

Family Relationships

a mother
a father
a grandmother
a grandfather
a daughter
a son
a sister
a brother
a husband
a wife
a grandson
a granddaughter

Verbs

go (to a rock concert,
    for a walk)
hang (up)
order (to)
press
spell
walk
watch

*Commands
(Imperatives)*

choose a partner
close the door
go to the board
open your books
raise your hand
sit down
stand up

Possessive Adjectives

my
your
his
her
its
our
their

Adjectives

broken
hungry
late

Adverbs

please
ready
really

Wh- words

how

Preposition

about

Expressions

Good idea.
Let's go.
Let's not (go out).
No problem.

Unit 4

Nouns

a ball
a car
a corner
dinner
directions
exercise
a gas station
homework
a house
a light
lunch
work

Verbs

call
can't
do
fix
give
make
miss
play
run
turn

*Present Continuous:
Present Participles*

calling
delivering
doing
driving
exercising
fixing
leaving
living
making
serving
talking
watching
working

Adjectives

busy
late
lost
left
right
sorry

Adverbs

later
left
right

Ordinal Numbers

first
second
third
fourth
fifth
sixth
seventh
eighth
ninth
tenth
eleventh
twelfth

Object Pronouns

me
you
him
her
it
us
them

Unit 5

Nouns

Places to Work

an office
a restaurant
a store
a supermarket

Fields of Study

art
business

computers
dance
journalism
math
medicine
music
a detective

Verbs

Simple Present Tense

find/finds
get/gets

has/have
like/likes
love/loves
study/studies
teach/teaches
work/works
worry/worries

Negative Form

does not/doesn't
do not/ don't

Adjectives

difficult
easy
exciting
fun
hard
impossible
interesting
missing

Other

a lot

Unit 6

Nouns

an appointment
breakfast
a date
a dating service
help
a meeting
a patient
a problem
weekdays

Nouns Describing Illness

a backache
a cough
a fever
a headache
a sore throat
a toothache

Parts of the Body

an ankle
an arm
a back
an elbow
a hand
a knee
a shoulder
a wrist

Sports

baseball
basketball
soccer
tennis
volleyball

Verbs

be going to
hurt

leave
need

Adjectives

bored
dizzy
excited
nervous
tired
worried

Adverbs of Frequency

always
occasionally
often
never
rarely

seldom
sometimes
usually

Prepositions

at
from
in the
out of

Expressions

Gosh.
Good bye.
Thank you.
You're welcome.

Unit 7

Nouns

a bank
a dance
evening
a minute

Activities

biking
dancing
fishing

hiking
Roller-blading
skateboarding
swimming

Courses of Study

calculus
chemistry
English
history

Verbs

can/can't
dance
have, has, have to,
　　has to
help
play

Adjectives

hard
other

Adverbs

earlier
later

Expressions

Good idea.
Please?
Sorry.
Thanks a million.

Unit 8

Nouns

Shopping and Clothing

a bathing suit
a belt
a bikini
a blouse
boots
boxer shorts
a bra
briefs
clothing
a coat
a department store
a dress
a dress shirt
gloves
a jacket
loafers

the men's department
mittens
a nightgown
pajamas
panty hose
panties
pants
a raincoat
running shoes
sandals
shoes
shorts
a size
a skirt
sleepwear
slippers
socks
a sport shirt
a suit
a sweater
a tie

a T-shirt
an umbrella
an undershirt
underwear
a windbreaker
the women's
     department

Colors

beige
black
brown
blue
gray
green
orange
pink
purple
red
white
yellow

Adjectives

any
much
some
that
these
this
those

Pronouns

one
ones

Expressions

Excuse me.
How can I help you?
Right this way.
You're kidding!

Unit 9

Nouns

last week
last weekend
today
yesterday

*Social and Business
Relationships*

an assistant
the boss
a boyfriend
fiancé(e)s

a girlfriend
a husband
neighbors
a partner
roommates
a wife

Adjectives

familiar

Verbs

look
know
was

were
wasn't
weren't

Possessive Pronouns

mine
yours
his
hers
ours
their

Wh- words

where
why

Expressions

by the way
Don't worry.
go Dutch
I can afford it.
I'm sorry about that.
It's not fair.
No way!
oops
That's OK.
would you like to

Unit 10

Nouns

candy
cookies
mail

Adverb

back

Verbs

did not
didn't
sound

Regular Past Forms

played
practiced
studied

Irregular Past Forms

came
did
felt
found
forgot
got
grew
had

heard
knew
made
met
said
saw
told
took
thought
went

Past Time Expressions

a few days ago
a little while ago
last month
last week
twenty minutes ago
yesterday

Expressions

Guess who?

Simple Past Tense of Irregular Verbs

Base Form	Simple Past	Base Form	Simple Past
be	was, were	leave	left
become	became	let	let
begin	began	lose	lost
break	broke	make	made
bring	brought	meet	met
buy	bought	put	put
can	could (for ability only)	quit	quit
catch	caught	read	read
choose	chose	ride	rode
come	came	run	ran
cut	cut	say	said
do	did	see	saw
drink	drank	sell	sold
drive	drove	send	sent
eat	ate	sing	sang
fall	fell	sit	sat
feel	felt	sleep	slept
fight	fought	speak	spoke
fly	flew	stand	stood
forget	forgot	steal	stole
get	got	take	took
give	gave	teach	taught
go	went	tell	told
grow	grew	think	thought
have	had	throw	threw
hear	heard	understand	understood
hold	held	wake	woke, waked
hurt	hurt	win	won
keep	kept	write	wrote
know	knew		

Irregular Noun Plurals

Singular Form	Plural Form	Singular Form	Plural Form
child	children	person	people
foot	feet	tooth	teeth
knife	knives	wife	wives
life	lives	woman	women
man	men		

Spelling Rules for the Present Participle

If the base form ends in a silent *-e:* Drop the *-e* and add *-ing.*

make   +   -ing   =   making

If the base form ends in a single vowel + a single consonant (except *w, x,* and *y*): Double the consonant and add *-ing.*

run   +   -ing   =   running
mix   +   -ing   =   mixing

Add *-ing* to all other base forms

sleep   +   -ing   =   sleeping
wash   +   -ing   =   washing